# Abraham: The Last Jew

## By

## Mark Carp

To Stan,
All the best—
Always!

Mark Carp

ISBN: 1-4033-9104-1 (e-book)
ISBN: 1-4033-9105-X (Paperback)

Library of Congress Control Number: 2002095524

This book is printed on acid free paper.

Printed in the United States of America
Bloomington, IN

Cover by Bennett Grizzard

1stBooks - rev. 04/12/03

# Acknowledgments

I'd like to thank Nikki Traino and Dr. Bruce Sindler for their suggestions involving the creation of a piece of sculpture and a medical procedure, respectively.

I'd also like to thank Janet Kozlay for typing the manuscript and for offering editing and grammatical suggestions, and Nancy Carp and Barbara Harr for reviewing the manuscript.

I'd additionally like to thank the Baltimore Hebrew College for providing assistance with phonetic spellings of Yiddish and Hebrew words and interpretations of Jewish history.

Finally, I'd like to thank Random House for allowing me to use a section of *Portnoy's Complaint* and *Cliffs Notes* for allowing me to use three phrases from its interpretation of the *Merchant of Venice*.

God forbid the past should be prologue.

Mark Carp

# Dedication

To my father, Maynard L. Carp, who gave me my will.

To my grandmother, Rose Krakowitz, who gave me my soul.

To my grandfather, Herman Krakowitz, who took me to the Baltimore Orioles' games.

# Chapter I

## Alive

It was 2250 and he didn't know how many Jews were alive. It happened again, a mass murder. This time not in the millions, but in the tens of millions.

He began to search the death camps to find his co-religionists. Instead he found carcasses piled on top of one another, like discarded metal scraps that had been warped and bent.

The sight sickened him.

He made his way to the big city, Ugograd, which had once been a hub of Jewish life.

The fighting had stopped, so he felt safe.

He was emotionally wounded as images and questions tortured him. "Why again a mass murder?" he asked himself. "Why again?" he repeated.

Levi Bushkin's features were dark and his hair wavy. His nose was Semitically curved, and his height was five feet ten inches, with his weight of one hundred and eighty pounds spread in nice proportion over his frame. Instantly recognized as a Jew, Bushkin, as he walked the city streets, was gawked at by some— a Semite amid a sea of non-Jews. Others, however, turned their heads, ashamed to face a survivor--perhaps the only one--of yet another "final solution."

Bushkin soon made his way to a large church, a granite and stone edifice that was tall and stark looking. He walked through the lobby and made his way through a narrow, poorly lit corridor. He came to

Father Yosef Vagins' office. He didn't have an appointment but said to Vagins' assistant that he wanted to discuss some religious matters.

He was told Vagins was busy.

Bushkin said he would wait. Prior to the war, Vagins had been an important writer on theological matters. His books and numerous articles continually compared Judaism to Christianity in terms of worship, monotheism, comparability of observances, and the embracing of a common ethic.

As he waited for the meeting, Bushkin's mind was restless. He wanted to discuss genocide in the following context: If there was this comparability between Christians and Jews, why were Christians in the vanguard of genocidal movements against the Jews? After all, Christ was a Jew and a rabbi. In effect, then, Jews and Christians were descendants of the same family tree. They were related historically and biologically.

Bushkin's musings were interrupted as Vagins' assistant said he would see him. The Father's office was a few feet from the waiting area. As he entered, he noted the spare furnishings and a large, bronze, highly polished crucifix that dominated the rear wall of a windowless office. On two other walls were pictures of the crucifixion and the Madonna and Child.

As Bushkin walked to Vagins' desk, he made his way over a large area rug. He and Vagins introduced themselves. The two exchanged a quick, mechanical handshake. Bushkin then settled in a large, comfortable leather chair and the two began to talk.

A troubled Bushkin asked the Father, "What do you think God had intended for the Jews?"

Vagins was uneasy. Following another Holocaust, who could offer a satisfactory interpretation. He didn't answer.

After a pause, Bushkin asked, "Why the Jews? Why always the Jews? Why were they always society's scapegoats?

"Why was it that it was the Christians who led the unspeakable recriminations?

"Had God abandoned the Jews?"

Vagins pondered the questions, but only answered the latter one.

"God had not abandoned the Jews," said Vagins. "Man had. Destruction of a people cannot be God's will. We are God's creatures," Vagins concluded. "God didn't want his creations destroyed."

"If Abraham was the first monotheist and was dutiful and paid homage to God, why was it that his progeny suffered?" Bushkin asked.

"People are misguided," Vagins answered.

"If Christians are obeisant to Christ, and they respect his teachings, why do they murder Jews?" replied Bushkin.

"They are not true Christians," answered Vagins.

"Then can what has happened to the Jews again and again be explained in any kind of theological sense?" asked Bushkin.

Vagins hesitated and then said emphatically, "No."

Bushkin felt he had explanations without answers. But hadn't that always been the case?

Pogrom, expulsion, bondage, holocaust, and a final solution--one consequence worse than another. Who could make sense of this? Let the theologians and

3

social scientists try. No one could properly put such outcomes in a meaningful context.

It was just random stupidity and unfathomable violence.

To Bushkin the greater wonder was the Jews of Abraham, Moses, and Einstein were always undermined by the antagonists: the Pharaoh, Torquemada, and Hitler.

Moreover, Bushkin knew Jews would never have committed genocide against Christians.

Then why Jewish achievement and destruction?

Bushkin knew instinctively that he would never understand the problem in a theological context. Rather, he chose to formulate in the most general terms: The Semitic minority because of its accomplishments had always been too visible, sometimes to its own detriment. Therefore, when the demagogues emerged, who but the "Christ killers" to undermine. They were an easy target--though powerful, they were small in number and easy to isolate and destroy. Accept it for what it is--man's inhumanity to man--nothing more, nothing less.

Bushkin now knew other explanations--religious and secular-- would not suffice.

Therefore, whoever remained as a Jew--the few living and their progeny--would have their own perpetual cross to bear. This would never change, as the reading, and now the living of history, had educated him.

# Chapter II

# The Search

Bushkin slept well that night. He awoke in a nondescript room in a hotel that was adjacent to the once-thriving business district. When he arose from his bed, he entered the bathroom and looked in the mirror, but didn't see his face. Instead, as he began to lather up for his daily shave, he saw images of his people being herded off to the death camps. The specter sickened him.

He then finished shaving and smacked some cold water against his face. As he did, the desperate images disappeared. Bushkin hurried downstairs and had a quick breakfast. He promptly paid his bill and checked out. Bushkin walked three blocks to a railroad station and boarded a train heading east. Seven hundred and fifty miles from Ugograd, he exited at Tashni, a moderate-sized city framed by mountains to the east. He began to hike up a mountain approximately five thousand feet in height. Bushkin surmised that he would likely find Jews in hiding who were unaware that the fighting had stopped.

Sewers, mountains, attics, woods, and disguises had always been the temporary refuge of Jews on the run. As one who believed that the past is prologue, Bushkin knew instinctively that he could expect to find his co-religionists, if not in this mountain chain, certainly in other formations.

Nearly halfway up the peak, he came across a small flat area which was partially sheltered by overhanging vegetation and a rock formation that protruded from the mountain. Bushkin calculated that this area could be a natural sanctuary. He then noticed that some thick branches had been newly broken and some dirt seemed to have been recently disturbed. He decided to wait, expecting someone to return.

He sat down and leaned his back against a rock. As he did, he began to contemplate the war and its aftermath. His parents were murdered, as were his brother, grandparents, aunts, uncles, cousins, and likely all his Jewish friends and colleagues. At thirty-three years old, he was the only one in his family left. Moreover, as he knew, there was a world-wide destruction of Jewry. In the Americas and Europe, the Jews had been rounded up and destroyed. Israel had been bombed to the point where it was believed only a few had survived.

The world-wide demagogues had had their day as they cast the Jews as the international bankers in conspiracy; the people who controlled the media and polluted the minds of the masses; the ones who made nations adopt a pro-Israel strategy; the group who, in spite of its small numbers, dominated too much of life: the media, medicine, the arts, government, business and science. Even America's black preachers had condemned his co-religionists as the devil's merchants who overcharged the residents of the inner-cities. Never mind that it was the Jews who were in the vanguard of the Civil Rights movement some three hundred years before and also supported the NAACP. No, the demagogues and their complicit stupidity, along with their powerful armies, had again had their moment. What geniuses, he thought. First they kill the Jews as a pretense for going to war, then the nations kill each other until they get tired and then they sue for peace. Of course the leaders tell us we fight to preserve our nationalism, our nativism, our Americanism, our Europeanism, even our way-of-life "ism." It sounds so good in speech, but it is so barbaric in consequence.

Bushkin's thoughts were suddenly interrupted as he heard some tree limbs move. He became alarmed. Through the branches he saw an image. As it approached, he got up.

A woman pushed the final limbs away and emerged into the area where Bushkin stood. At first he was startled.

She seemed poised.

"I am Sasha Liebowitz," she said.

His eyes were immediately drawn to a gold chain that hung loosely around her neck. On it was attached a golden Star of David that resided just below the base of her neck.

Next Bushkin's eyes were drawn to Liebowitz's face. She was darkly complected with high cheek bones, deep-set eyes and raven-colored hair that hung loosely about her shoulders. Her features titillated him. He always confessed to being aroused by what he called "gorgeous Semitic features." Though he occasionally had dated shiksas, whom he deemed as cute and nothing more, he was inevitably drawn back to the dark, deep-set beauty of his co-religionists. Sasha stood about five feet five inches and weighed approximately one hundred twenty-five pounds. Her figure--the bustline, waist and hips--was beautifully proportioned; her age seemed to approach thirty.

After his eyes completed their quick inspection, he introduced himself. "I am Levi Bushkin," he said. "How did you get here?"

"I was taken to a camp with approximately three hundred others at Folensk, one hundred seventy-five miles east of here. I was at the end of a human chain, and I turned and started walking. I expected to be shot, and I wouldn't have cared if I had. My family and relatives were all dead, as was my fiance.

"Some people may have interpreted my defiance as bravery. Instead, it was desperation. I didn't care if I lived or died.

"I walked two miles to the road. I hitched a ride to Tashni. The driver saw my Star of David and didn't say a word. If the driver was found to be harboring a Jew, it was a crime that was punishable by death. The driver was a martyr, and I didn't even know his name."

"How did you get here, Levi?"

"Well, the war ended."

"It did?" said Sasha.

"Yes," said Bushkin, "four days ago. I was the last of my group living. I was supposed to be murdered. If the war had gone on another day, I would have been dead.

"With the peace, we have received amnesty. In the cities we are no longer hunted like animals, rounded up, incarcerated in death camps and murdered. Now our antagonists look at us, sometimes blankly, sometimes in shame. One day they hunt you; the next day they stare at you, even greeting you with a mechanical hello. This is civilization? This is barbaric. This is madness."

Sasha began to cry out inconsolably. "Why again?" she shrieked. "Why again?"

"The mob has a life of its own," replied Bushkin. "For us, when mobocracy ends, our life can begin. People are fools, and their stupidity becomes the tool of the mob. We are an easy target, small in number, though powerful in influence. So it was easy to blame the Jews for fictitious wrongs, surround us and murder us. Hasn't it always been this way!"

The two then stared into each other's eyes, and embraced so as to comfort one another in their hour of bewilderment and torment.

The embrace ended quickly.

The two decided to spend the night in an area where Liebowitz had slept. It was about ten yards from the flat area where they had met, an impromptu shelter that nature had miraculously cut out of some rock. In this edifice, the couple was removed from the elements. The two dined on berries that Liebowitz had foraged from nearby.

Now in the dark, Bushkin lay on one side of the shallow cave, Liebowitz on the other.

Though tired, he kept thinking about Sasha. He loved her looks, and he thought she was very mature and poised. He didn't know anything about her, but in his few waking moments Bushkin began to probe his imagination. He pictured her as a professional woman from a nice family who had a strong sense of dignity and self-worth. This specter intrigued him. He always enjoyed testing his intuitions--his gut reactions--rather than initially asking. It was a little game he liked to play. He was more often right than wrong. He felt very relaxed, more so than at any time in the past year--the period of the roundup, the Holocaust and the war. He was soon asleep and slept soundly.

The next morning, about 6 a.m., Bushkin awoke. Moments later Liebowitz got up. The two exchanged awkward glances and each issued a faint smile at the other. Each found the other attractive, and both found comfort in the other's company.

The two took turns washing at a nearby stream using soap and toothpaste that Liebowitz had taken to the death camp and had husbanded during her isolation.

About 7 a.m. the two had breakfast, a repeat of the berries from the night before. Following eating, Bushkin asked Liebowitz, "What did you do before the war?"

"I was a doctor," she said.

"What kind?"

"A surgeon."

"I'm impressed," said Bushkin, smiling.

Each began to laugh.

"And you?" said Sasha, continuing to laugh.

"I am a college professor. I teach classic literature."

"Oy," said Sasha.

"Oy?" replied Bushkin.

"I always thought all literature professors were crazy," laughed Sasha.

"Why?"

"God-forbid you could read a story and enjoy it. No, there were always hidden meanings: symbolism, irony, sexual implications, and on, and on, and on. If the writers were really that complex, they all would have had nervous breakdowns by the end of Chapter III."

Bushkin continued his unrestrained laughter.

"I must admit," he said, "we do make fools of ourselves . . . sometimes."

"Sometimes, Levi."

"I get your point," he said as his face maintained its unrestrained smile and he tried to control his laughter.

"And you?" said Bushkin. "How about you? I bet to you life was nothing but a series of be here, go there, clip the coupon, watch for the sales, make your deposits, and work, work, work. I'm sure you even knew the amount of money you had in your checking account to the dollar."

"To the penny," she said, only half-jokingly.

"Oh," she continued. "I bet you're a real romantic, always quoting pithy literary lines to your dates over candlelight and wine. And at the door you'd say, 'Parting is such sweet sorrow.' And when you did, I'm sure your date said, 'These are the best of times and the worst of times,' with no doubt an emphasis on the latter."

"And you," he replied. "I bet your idea of a beautiful evening is eating Chinese food out of cartons while in your curlers."

With that, the two concluded their repartee. Each had enjoyed it immensely. They had probed, contested and cajoled. And they found each other's company to their liking. Each loved being reduced to a stereotype, a cliche.

They now knew they would have to leave their mountain refuge to return to a world that had condemned their religion and had murdered their co-religionists.

By mid-morning they began their descent. Twenty minutes later they were down the mountain and outside of Tashni. Bushkin and Liebowitz said nothing during their descent.

Now they entered Tashni, where they faced an unsure and, at best, a fearful future. Life, they knew, could be very cruel.

# Chapter III

# Can There be Life After Death?

Bushkin and Sasha entered Tashni. Bushkin remembered the town once had a Jewish quarter, between five and ten thousand people, he thought. He recalled that diamond cutting was an occupation indigenous to this section.

In the town's center square, Bushkin headed to where he thought the Jewish quarter was, to the northwest of the town center. As he and Sasha walked, the streets began to narrow and changed to cobblestone, and the pavement's reduced width caused them to walk single file with Bushkin in the lead. Too, the buildings became taller, three and four stories, and narrower in frontage, to about fifteen feet. The northwest was an older section with the buildings dating from the fifteenth century.

"This must have been a center of Talmudic learning and scholarship," he told Sasha.

The images of the white-bearded rabbis dressed in dark clothing appeared to him along with their young students with yarmulkes and curled sidelocks. "I bet the cheder was there," he told Sasha as he pointed to a windowless building with a faded white color that had a barely discernible Star of David that he thought was originally painted blue.

As they walked around the corner, they came to a synagogue, Bnai Jacob. They opened the unlocked

13

door and walked in. They approached the altar and opened the door where the Torahs were kept. Several encased in a white silk covering were discolored by red markings that appeared to be randomly made.

"That is blood," said Sasha upon closer examination.

They finished their inspection and took one of the blood-soaked Torahs. They wrapped it carefully and left the building.

As they proceeded down the street to a section of shops, they walked to avoid the broken glass of the store windows.

"A repeat of Kristallnacht, no doubt," said Bushkin.

"It's bad enough they murder and pillage," said Sasha, "but why do they have to make such statements?"

"They're animals," replied Bushkin. "Killing isn't enough. They don't even have enough dignity to do their reprehensible deeds and leave. They think like a mob, act like a mob, and kill like a mob."

He then raised his voice to a level of intense anger as his face began to redden with rage. "There is not enough justice anywhere for the bastards," he told Sasha as his voice shook from emotion.

"Justice," said Sasha, "the only justice they deserve is to be murdered in retribution. They deserve the same justice they gave us. Justice is for the civilized."

The two retraced their steps to the town center, with Bushkin holding the newly wrapped Torah, whose scrolls were visible through the wrapping.

In the town center, they were approached by a couple. "I am Simon Leventhal," he said, "and this is my wife, Ruth."

"I am Levi Bushkin," he replied, "and this is a friend of mine, Sasha Liebowitz."

Recognizing Bushkin and Sasha as Jews, Leventhal said, "Ruth and I lived here. I had a machine shop south of town. Some of what we manufactured were munition parts used by the Defense Department. I wonder how much of my manufactured goods were used in killing us."

"Stop tormenting yourself," said Ruth.

"This is some end," said Simon, "My people are murdered; my family is gone; and we are supposed to be the chosen ones, the people of the covenant.

"If we are the chosen ones, I'd hate to see who came in second," he chided as he looked skyward and scolded God for what he thought was betrayal.

Then, staring at Bushkin, he said: "I revered God; I thanked him for my life and prosperity; and I observed the Shabbos and attended services regularly. This is how my faith has been rewarded.

"My life is broken."

"Do you plan to remain in Tashni?" interrupted Bushkin.

"No," replied Leventhal, "it would be too hard. I would see ghosts everywhere."

Then Bushkin abruptly excused himself and Sasha from the Leventhals, who remained at the town center.

"That was rude," said Sasha. "Don't you have compassion? Couldn't you have at least listened? How many of us are left?

"Why don't you go back and apologize?"

"I don't want to, Sasha. My life is in torment too. At some point I have to move away from this Holocaust and its aftermath. There is only so much I can take and listen to. I'm not a rabbi making rounds in order to provide comfort. My life has been a hell for the last six months. Who is going to listen to me?"

"I'm sorry," said Sasha.

"Don't be sorry. It is just that the events are so overwhelming, there will be times my responses will be misunderstood. I am not perfect."

"Let's leave Tashni," said Sasha.

Neither said a word as they walked to the train station six blocks away.

"Instead of buying a train ticket," said Bushkin at the station, "let's rent a car. It's Sunday, we can get a good deal and being alone will give us a chance to talk more privately, and maybe get to know each other better."

"Why should I want to get to know you better, Levi?"

"I am afraid you're stuck with me for a while."

"Stuck, Levi? I don't want to be 'stuck.' I need someone to lean on. I need someone with strength. I need help."

"I need the same, Sasha. I'm no hero. I'm not your prince in shining armor."

"At least you're honest," Sasha replied.

"Honest," he snapped. "This isn't a time for verbal sparring. If we can't talk directly to one another now, we will never be able to."

"You remind me of Yuri," Sasha interrupted.

"Who?"

"Yuri was my fiance."

"I should have guessed."

"You should have," said Sasha with an edge in her voice, as if to make Bushkin feel guilty for missing the obvious segue.

"Look," he snapped, "if you have something to say, say it. Don't try to coax things out of me. I am not good at game playing.

"Don't erect a wall between us. Don't play mind games. Remember you told me you thought all college literature professors were crazy with the use of symbolism. So if I'm crazy, don't contribute to my insanity by talking symbolically."

Before Sasha could fashion what would have undoubtedly been a prickly response, a man behind the rental counter shouted, "Next."

Bushkin walked to the counter, laid the Torah down and asked about terms.

He quickly signed a rental agreement, picked up a set of keys and walked outside to the car. Sasha followed. He carefully placed the Torah in the trunk. She got in first. He followed.

He pulled out and maneuvered the car onto the high-speed expressway. He turned on the radio.

"Turn it off," said Sasha.

"Why?"

"I want to talk to you."

"Okay, so talk."

"Can't you be nicer?"

"Get to the point," he demanded. "I can read you like a book. You want to talk about Yuri."

"So if you know, why can't you at least be gracious?"

"I told you, if you have something to say, say it. Did you love him?"

"Are you jealous?"

"Jealous of what, someone I didn't know?" he said agitatedly.

"Okay, tell me about Yuri."

"You're making me angry, Levi."

"Tell me about Yuri or shut up."

"Okay."

"What was he like?"

"He was the love of my life."

"I should have known. Now I'm going to ask you again: What was he like?"

"Like no one else I ever knew, including you."

"You have one more chance. Tell me what he was like, or we're going to drop this conversation."

"Okay. I loved him deeply. I have a tremendous sense of loss. He was like no one I had ever met before."

"How so?"

"He was so different from the others I knew and dated."

"Get on with it."

"He had instincts."

"Instincts?"

"I mean he had a rough sense of integrity. He was intense, and he could be a real loner. He didn't need to be part of the crowd. Instead, he could look at things with an analytical criticalness."

"Explain."

"Well, he was in finance, and he was an expert in stocks and bonds. When things were going well he tended to become very critical. 'Values are crazy,' he would tell me. 'This will never last.' On the other hand, when things were at their depths and it appeared that the sun would never again rise, he tended to be the most animated. 'What values,' he would tell me, because that's when he bought.

"He had two sides--he could be a real screamer who carried on like a meshugena--and then there was his social side--he loved classical music, literature, sporting events, and, most of all, he loved me. At work he would practically rip someone's throat out over a sixteenth of a point. Yet the same night we would go to the symphony and if the orchestra was playing some particularly beautiful passages of Gershwin, Rachmaninoff or Tchaikovsky, he would tend to become choked up, even teary eyed.

"'It is so beautiful,' he would tell me in a voice that had grown soft and had become hoarse with emotion.

"He also liked art."

"What kind?"

"Rembrandt and Michelangelo were his favorites."

"Why?"

"He raved about Rembrandt's use of light and shadow to produce what he called a 'rarified and exquisite beauty.' As for Michelangelo, we saw the Moses in Rome. Yuri just stood there and stared."

"Did he comment on the horns?"

"Not really. He was aware they were there, but he focused on the anatomy. He said he 'never saw such an idealized yet accurate and structurally perfect depiction of anatomy in his life.' I remember as we left he turned to me and said, 'If the damn thing gets up and walks out, I won't be surprised.' To him, that was art of the highest order."

"Go on," insisted Bushkin.

"As to his tastes in literature," she said, "he loved Jewish writers: Philip Roth, Isaac Bashevis Singer, and Stanley Elkin among them. He was also a huge admirer of Ernest Hemingway.

"And he loved to laugh. I can't tell you how many times he saw the same Marx Brothers and Woody Allen movies, and he had to see everything by Neil Simon. And in his own way, he had a beautiful sense of humor. Once when he was at an intellectual gathering and the conversation turned to the greatest minds in the history of mankind, he was told the group was evenly divided between DaVinci and Einstein. A member of the group said, 'Fromkin, what is your opinion?'

"'As for me,' he said, 'I'll always be partial to Harpo Marx.'

"Believe or not, he was also a fine musician who played the piano beautifully. He played with tremendous feeling, and his repertoire included everything from classical to contemporary.

"He was also a great influence on me. Whenever I became afraid of the future, he would encourage me with this saying: 'You can be scared, but you can't be afraid.' It was his way of saying it's time to move on.

"Not that he didn't have his blind spots, he did. But when I was 'blind,' he could see for me and vice versa.

"And the crazy thing was, we were the most total of opposites. Even though we liked so many of the same things, we did so for totally different reasons."

"Maybe one day I can be your totally opposite significant other, Sasha."

"Don't be cute," she replied.

"I'm not." With that, he leaned over and kissed her lightly on the cheek. She did not respond.

"We will be in Ugograd this evening. This may be a good place to stop and settle down."

"Why?"

"It has the University that is affiliated with a hospital," he said. "Maybe I can get a job at the University and you at the hospital."

"Levi, I'm scared. Whatever you do, don't leave me. I want to stay with you."

"I'm scared, too. Maybe it's best to remember what your late fiance told you."

"What's that?"

"You can be scared, but you mustn't be afraid."

With that the two knew it was time to face an uncertain future.

# Chapter IV

# Ugograd

Ugograd was a big city. Its population was currently six million, and it previously had a representative proportion of Jewish residents, about a million before the war. Its architecture was visibly urban, as its buildings were tall and rectangular. Ugograd's streets and sidewalks always seemed to support an incomprehensible amount of activity.

It was also an important port city.

Bushkin frequented the city often. Sasha had only been there once, when she was twelve years old and had spent four days with her family on a vacation.

As Bushkin entered Ugograd, traffic began to slow to a crawl, even though it was late Sunday evening. His car was now part of a vehicular line where progress seemed imperceptible. He became agitated because of the tie-up and began to tap the steering wheel impatiently with a ring that was on his pinky finger.

After a few minutes of tapping, Sasha asked him to stop.

"That's irritating," she said.

"I hate lines, Sasha."

Finally, the knot of traffic began to disappear, and after thirty minutes of little movement, car traffic began to resume at close to a normal speed.

"We should try to get a short-term lease on an apartment," he told Sasha. "There are several thousand units near the old Jewish section." Bushkin then headed toward the apartment complexes and parked in front of the Sagrev Arms.

It was an older building, approximately fifty stories high.

He pulled up in front and asked the doorman if an employee was available to rent them a unit.

The doorman said yes.

Bushkin went into the trunk and took out the Torah, still carefully wrapped in brown paper.

Bushkin, carrying the Torah, preceded Sasha into the building. They met the rental agent. Bushkin laid the Torah down gently.

"I don't want things to be misunderstood," Sasha told the rental agent. "I want a two-bedroom furnished apartment."

"I don't want things to be misunderstood either," said Bushkin. "We'll take a two-bedroom with a den, only if the den is big enough to be converted into a third bedroom. I don't want people to get the wrong idea, you know."

With that, Sasha's eyes narrowed as her stare turned angry and her manner became abrasive. She then pursed her lips together and walked quickly from Bushkin, accelerating her steps as she moved.

As she got to the door, Bushkin asked sarcastically: "Where are you going, doctor?" making sure to give the "d" a hard emphasis so as to add to his intended sarcasm.

She slammed the door as she walked out. She stood by the side of the car, waiting for him.

Instead, he signed the rental agreement and carried the Torah to the elevator and made his way to the twenty-fifth floor, to unit 2507. She returned to the lobby a few minutes later expecting to find him there. The rental agent advised her of what unit he was in. She took the elevator to the twenty-fifth floor and knocked impatiently on the door.

"Go away," he told her. "I don't want people to get the wrong idea, doctor."

"Let me in," she said.

"What will people say, doctor?"

"If you don't let me in, I'll . . ." and suddenly the door opened.

"You'll what, doctor?"

She walked in. He smiled at her. She began to laugh; so did he.

"I'm tired," he said. "I'm going to bed."

"Can't we talk?" she asked.

"We better go to our rooms. We don't want people to get the wrong idea, doctor."

Bushkin washed up in the bathroom in his room and turned off the light, preparing to fall asleep quickly.

Several minutes later he heard a knock at the door.

"Is that you, doctor?" he asked.

"You know who it is. Please let me in. I want to talk to you."

"Okay, doctor," he said as he unlocked the door.

"Would you lie with me, Levi?" she said softly. He took her by the arm and escorted her to the bed. As the two lay down, he began to stroke her hair, rub her back, and kiss her lightly around the cheek and neck.

She became titillated, as did he. They engaged in foreplay and made love.

After they consummated their lovemaking, she said, "Things are happening too fast, Levi."

"We are two people," he responded, "who are caught up in a swirl of events that we have little control over. As a result, things are magnified and intensified far out of proportion. We are two fairly normal people caught up in abnormal times."

After a pause, Bushkin said, "You can go now, doctor."

"I want to stay with you, Levi."

"Even if people get the wrong idea, doctor?"

"I won't tell if you won't, professor."

"Okay, doctor."

He held her in his arms and her head rested on his. The two soon fell asleep in each other's arms.

As they awoke the next morning, she began to stare at him. He smiled.

"I'm glad you found me," she said.

"I'm glad I found you too, Sasha. Two days ago I didn't know you. Now I think I love you. A month ago I didn't think I'd be alive. Now I have you."

"That was so sweet," she said.

"I didn't intend for this to happen this way, but I wanted to tell you what was in my heart, Sasha."

"It is still sweet," she replied.

"We have to get on with living. These are impossible times," Bushkin said. "I'm going to the University today to inquire about a job. I would suggest you go to University Hospital to do the same. We will have to buy clothes, and we need groceries."

"I really don't cook," she said.

"I really do eat," he replied, "so you'll have to learn. This morning I'm going to walk around the old Jewish section before I go to the University this afternoon."

"I want to go with you."

"Let me be alone," he responded.

"Please let me go with you."

"No, Sasha. I'll be back no later than 5 p.m.

"I, I, I" he stammered.

"What?" she asked.

"I love you, Sasha."

"I love you too, Levi."

"By the way," she said, "what should we do with the extra bedroom?"

"I guess you can tell people you've just rented a one-bedroom and two-den apartment," winking at her as he said it. She smiled.

He left the building and walked to where the rental car was parked. He drove it around the corner to where the rental agency was and returned it.

He got out and proceeded to the old Jewish section. His mood began to sadden.

# Chapter V

# Here Was Once Judaica

He looked up as he entered the old Jewish section. He saw the signs: Ashkenazi Brothers Appliances, Blum's Deli, Sandler's Department Store, Minkove's Menswear, Fruchtman's Ladies Apparel, Samuel's Shoes, The Hebrew Gift Shop. It was 10 a.m., the start of the business day on Tramin Street, the section's retail center. However, the metal store grates stayed locked shut. The signs stayed unlit. The people were absent.

Tramin Street was ghost-like. Where there was once vibrancy, there was now stillness. Where there were once shoppers who formed human chains, there were now empty pavements where litter accumulated depressingly. Where there were cars that probed for openings, there was only an occasional automobile now, that came by at speeds that would have been unanticipated eighteen months ago.

In the middle of the block he came to Yuri's, an eatery. He walked in and sat down. "Can I help you?" said an older man stationed behind the counter.

"Juice and coffee, please," said Bushkin.

"Yes, sir. Coming right up, sir," he replied.

"How's business?" Bushkin asked.

"Can't you see," said the counterman. "Since the Jews are gone, there is none: no merchants, no shoppers.

27

"Say," continued the counterman, "aren't you a Jew?"

"Yes," replied Bushkin.

"This was once a vibrant Jewish center," said the man.

"I know," said Bushkin. "I was in Ugograd often before the war. I always liked coming to Tramin Street. It was fun for me."

"Unless something changes soon," said the counterman, "I will have to close.

"All my Jewish customers are gone. It's so sad. You know," he said as he wiped away some tears, "many of my customers were regulars. They had become, how do you say, like mishpachah."

"That's right," said Bushkin, "mishpachah, like family."

"That's right," said the attendant, "family."

"There was Mrs. Goldberg. She made me crazy, but I loved her. She used to come in at 10 a.m. every morning and order the same thing: coffee and a bun. Every time I served her a bun, she said, 'I don't like the looks of that one. Let me see the tray.' So I'd go back, get the tray and lay it on the counter so she could choose one. She always picked from a dozen or so that were on the tray. She always picked the fattest one with the most raisins. It became our little ritual. I'd swear we had customers who came in just to watch us.

"Once when we were busy and packed three deep at the counter, she knew I wouldn't have time to go through our ritual: giving her a bun only to have her reject it and then pick from the tray which I had to bring up from the rear. So I said to her pointedly, 'Which one is it?'

"'You don't know?' she said. I said, 'Mrs. Goldberg, I'm not a mind reader.' She said, 'Yuri' (my name is Leonid), 'get me the fattest one with the most raisins. Can't you see I'm tired of watching you hold up your customers?' The customers, crowded, irritable, and in a hurry, and packed three deep at the counter, began to fall over themselves with laughter.

"I knew my customers. I knew from their children, grandchildren, weddings, anniversaries, and bar mitzvahs.

"The day I dreaded most was when I had to raise prices. You never heard such carrying on. 'You ought to be ashamed of yourself,' or 'What are you trying to do?' they would tell me. One even asked me, 'How do you sleep at night?' They would become indignant and some cursed me from under their breath.

"Yet, when my cook got sick and I couldn't pay him, the customers and merchants pitched in and paid his rent, grocery, and other bills until he got on this feet. That was what you call tzedakah."

"That's right," said Bushkin, "tzedakah--charity."

"Yet," said the counterman, "they never asked for the money to be repaid."

With that, Bushkin finished his coffee, paid his bill, and walked outside. Two blocks from Tramin Street, he came across a large synagogue, Ner Israel. Its doors were open. Bushkin walked into the imposing structure with its large floor area, high vaulted ceilings and its pristine white Stars of David mounted majestically in the glass windows two stories above the floor.

Bushkin approached a laborer who was removing rows of seating.

"What are you doing?" asked Bushkin.

"The city is taking the building, sir. It will become a public gymnasium. The basketball court will be laid here," as he pointed to a section in the middle of the floor. Bushkin didn't say a word. He decided to leave the Tramin Street area and walk to the University, about five blocks away. The day was clear and crisp, the kind he liked to walk in.

Ten minutes later he was on the large campus and saw signs for the Department of Literature. He entered the building and followed signs to the chairman of the department. He walked into the office.

"I would like to apply for a job," he told the receptionist. The woman, startled at Bushkin's Semitic features, excused herself and walked quickly back to see the head of the department, Vladimir Moscov.

Moscov walked into the receptionist's area. Bushkin got up and introduced himself.

Moscov asked him back to his office.

"Weren't you on the faculty at Remenov University?" he asked.

"Yes. How did you know?"

"I read some of your critiques in the <u>Literary Journal</u>. They were well done, well thought out, and well reasoned."

"Thank you, Dr. Moscov."

"So you are looking for a job?"

"Yes."

"Why did you come to Ugograd?"

"Where am I going to run?"

Moscov was uneasy over the reply and, unable to fashion a response, began to repeatedly clear his throat. After doing so three times, he told Bushkin of an opening.

"Dr. Nobacov is in ill health," he said. "It is highly improbable that he will be able to return. You take his course."

"And what is that?" replied Bushkin.

"Literature 300. It consists of the following books: For Whom the Bell Tolls by Hemingway, The Trial by Kafka, Death of a Salesman by Miller, and The Sound and the Fury by Faulkner."

"That's a rather eclectic twentieth-century assortment," said Bushkin pleasingly and in a tone that expressed his eagerness to return to the classroom.

"Oh, by the way," said Moscov. "There will be one more."

"What's that?" asked Bushkin.

"The Merchant of Venice," replied Moscov.

"But, sir," said Bushkin, "can we substitute for that?"

"No," said Moscov.

"But, sir."

"No," repeated Moscov.

"If you don't want the job, I will hire someone else."

"When do I start?"

"The semester starts next week. We look forward to having you on the staff."

"I hope you do," said Bushkin in a tone that expressed some uneasiness at teaching The Merchant of Venice.

"I am sure you will get along just fine," replied Moscov.

"See my assistant in the front of the office. She will have you fill out some forms and will give you a schedule."

"Thank you," said Bushkin as he left Moscov's office.

A few minutes later Moscov's assistant returned to his office. "Issue a press release to the Informant newspaper that Dr. Levi Bushkin has joined the staff," she was told.

"This will be interesting," she replied.

"Go ahead and do it," he snapped.

A few minutes later the press release was faxed to the Informant. It was placed on the desk of Olga Tereshnova, a young reporter. Tereshnova immediately was able to get Bushkin's phone number from the school, and she called him.

Sasha answered the phone.

"He's not in," she replied to Tereshnova, who asked to speak to him. "I will tell him you called. Leave me your number."

At 3 p.m. Bushkin returned.

Sasha greeted him at the door.

Bushkin kissed her lightly on the cheek.

"How did it go today?" he asked.

"Fine, Levi."

"How so?"

"The hospital hired me."

"So soon."

"Not soon enough. Since the murder of the Jewish doctors, there is a severe shortage. I told them I'll start on Monday."

"Maybe," said Bushkin, "you ought to consider a second career."

"What's that?"

"You ought to go to law school at night," he chided her.

Sasha, finding rueful humor in the statement, let out a short and unmistakably cynical laugh.

"By the way, Levi, you got a call from Olga Tereshnova. She is with the <u>Informant</u>."

"She must have heard that the University hired me to teach literature."

"Congratulations," said Sasha.

"I'm going out to buy clothes. I'll call her when I get back."

"We might as well go together," said Sasha. "We will also need groceries."

Bushkin waited until Tuesday morning to call back Tereshnova. The two agreed to an interview. They met on Tuesday on Tramin Street at 2 p.m. in front of Yuri's.

After the introduction, the two began to walk together along the vacant retail corridor.

Tereshnova asked, "How does it feel to be a survivor?"

"It's hard to be a survivor, Ms. Tereshnova."

"How so?"

"You begin to feel guilty about living. You ask yourself, 'Why did I survive when so many didn't?' They didn't deserve that fate, and I didn't deserve to live if so many had to die."

"What do you see as your future? Do you want to live as a Jew?"

"Yes, I will live as a Jew. I won't run from what I am. As to my secular future, I am returning to academia as a literature professor.

"Let's walk over here," he told Tereshnova.

They were soon in front of Ner Israel.

"This makes me very sad," he told her.

"Why?"

"The city is converting the synagogue into a gymnasium. This is wrong. This is a place of worship and Jewish learning, of Talmudic and Torah study. This is a place where you observed the High Holidays, Rosh Hashanah and Yom Kippur. This is where the cantor chanted Kol Nidre on Yom Kippur. This was where couples were married under the chupah and the groom broke the glass. This is where Jewish boys became bar mitzvahed and girls bat mitzvahed. This is breaking my heart."

"What can you do about it?"

"Nothing but talk about it," he replied.

"Demographers are estimating there may be as few as one hundred thousand Jews left in the world. What is your reaction?"

"It's unspeakable," he replied curtly.

Now back on Tramin Street and passing rows of vacant retail shops, Tereshnova asked, "Do you hope more 'survivors' migrate to Ugograd?"

"I hope so. There is usually strength in numbers. Hopefully we may be able to put together a community. However, you worry that many Jews will stay underground and eventually lose their identity."

"Isn't that analogous to what happened to the Marranos in Spain during and after the Inquisition?" Tereshnova asked.

"Yes, that is the proper analogy, Ms. Tereshnova."

"If a Jewish community were to grow, would you worry about outbreaks of anti-Semitism, physical and otherwise?"

"I always worry about the fools and their mobs."

"If a Jewish community grows, would you project yourself as a leader?"

"No. As Jews, we don't look to a leader. Jews, for the most part, are individualists and free thinkers who are capable of intellectually challenging the status quo. No matter what the issue--economics, government, religion, or law--Jews are all over the opinion spectrum."

"When I called, a woman answered the phone. Who is she?"

"Her name is Sasha Liebowitz. She is a doctor and also a Jew. She has just been employed at University Hospital."

"This article will appear in our national edition, Dr. Bushkin. Maybe you will get calls from your co-religionists who would like to settle in Ugograd."

"We'll see, Ms. Tereshnova. Let's go walk over to Yuri's and I'll buy you coffee."

As Bushkin and Tereshnova walked in, Leonid was behind the counter.

"Hello again," he said to Bushkin.

"Two coffees, please," said Bushkin.

"By the way," Leonid said, "I have given notice to my landlord. I'm closing at the end of the month. The Jews are gone and so am I."

# Chapter VI

# The Article

"Andrei, it's for you."

"Who is it?"

"Some reporter. She wants to speak to you."

"About what?"

"Take the phone," said Ludmilla, his wife.

"This is Andrei Traicov. Can I help you?"

"Yes, I'm Olga Tereshnova, a reporter with the Informant. A Jewish couple has moved into Ugograd. Do you wish to comment?"

"I thought they were all dead."

"No," replied Tereshnova, "demographers are estimating as few as one hundred thousand remain worldwide."

"No comment," said Traicov, as he hung up.

The newspaper article appeared the next day.

"Look at this, Ludmilla."

"What's it say?"

"Let me read," said Andrei.

"A Jewish couple, Levi Bushkin, Ph.D., and his acquaintance, Dr. Sasha Leibowitz, have taken up residence in Ugograd.

"Bushkin has recently been employed by the University where he will teach literature. Dr. Liebowitz is now a member of the staff at University Hospital.

"In spite of being a survivor of what historians are calling a 'second' Final Solution, Bushkin will maintain his faith and live openly as a Jew. He hopes that eventually the community can attract more Jewish survivors.

"He called the fact that demographers are estimating that as few as one hundred thousand Jews remain worldwide 'unspeakable.'"

"I can't read anymore," said Traicov. "Give me the phone."

"Sergei?"

"Yes."

"It's Andrei.

"They're back."

"Who?"

"The Jews."

"They're not all dead?"

"No, two have just moved to Ugograd."

"This will bear watching," said Sergei. "I will see you at our meeting next week. Good-bye."

"Ludmilla," said Andrei, "put that on the agenda of the National Organization." (National Organization, or NO, before and during the war had been an openly anti-Semitic organization and had assisted the government in the roundup of the Jews.)

In the western part of the country, Isadore Samonovich, a merchant, read the article with his wife, Yetta.

"You know, Yetta, this will be a fantastic opportunity. If I could lease the old Sandler's Department Store, that would give me the dominant location in the retail corridor. The property is on an excellent corner and has exceptional exposure. It is easily accessible. We could reopen under the old name. Everyone knew Sandler's and its motto: Your Bargains are Our Business. I bet I could rent the property for a percentage of sales. As to merchandise, I am sure I could stock the store on a consignment basis. This is a natural. It would be like having a license to print money. Hopefully, Ugograd will attract more Jews. You know it was one of the world's great Jewish centers, and think of all that business."

South of Ugograd the article was read by Tatyana Samuelson, an artist. She had survived the war by living in a sewer system and by coming out at night to forage for food, mostly from garbage cans in alleyways. She attended school in Ugograd, at the famous Art Institute. Prior to the war, she had gained a modicum of fame for her avant-garde impressionist paintings and sculptures. She loved to paint urban life, depicting figures that were outrageously large and angular in comparison to the urban landscape of sky-scraping buildings that sat on impossibly narrow streets. Her sculptures often featured body parts that were attractively disproportionate to one another. Her Atlas Holding the World depicts him with a pencil-thin waist from which his massively defined chest and then arms and shoulders flow. His handsome head has a robotic-square shape that seems to project incomprehensible strength. Atlas's legs are roundly muscular and are rigidly impervious to the earth's weight, which he carries heroically on his back.

Her forays into the world of the avant-garde often rankled the sedate world of the classicists. In some circles she was referred to as the "Jew artist."

She recalled Ugograd's old apartment buildings that were ribboned with windows, the kind that produced an abundance of natural light from which she liked to paint and sculpt. She loved the anonymity of the city, and admired its energy and pulse. For her, there would be subject matter aplenty in Ugograd.

Though a Jew by birth, Samuelson did not practice her religion. On the other hand, she never denied her origins.

North of the city, the story was read by Vasily Ginsberg. Prior to the war, he had gained a reputation for notorious financial dealings. As an investment banker/financier, he brought several companies public based on fictitious earnings. On one occasion, he went on trial for financial fraud, but with the aid of the country's most politically connected Jewish law firm, he was found innocent, much to the outrage of the country. His dealings had cost investors hundreds of millions of dollars. He also was a controlling shareholder in several companies and was said to have looted them, drawing outrageous compensation that often left those firms only marginally capitalized and on the edge of bankruptcy.

He survived the war by giving large bribes to high government officials in return for his safety. In some circles, he was referred to as the modern-day Shylock.

He was a tall man, six feet two inches in height, and was generously handsome with brown wavy hair and a beautiful bronze complexion that seemed to carry a luster. He was built exquisitely with wide shoulders and a narrow waist. Ginsberg had a manly grace, and when he walked into a room, people noticed and were drawn to him.

He had been married and divorced three times before the war. His last two mates were shiksa trophy wives, and his third wife, Sophia Natanya, had starred in several B-movies.

He had always wanted to settle in Ugograd, the seat of the country's finance. The stock and commodity exchanges were there, as were the most powerful investment bankers. To him, Ugograd was the nation's nerve center and a nexus to the financial power he would continue to covet.

"Look at this," said Sarah Potemkin to her husband, Yakov.

"What is it?"

"A Jewish couple has moved to Ugograd, Yakov."

"Let me read. Hmmm. A doctor and a professor. Maybe Ugograd will return someday as a Jewish mecca."

Before the war, Yakov Potemkin had been a prosperous lawyer in the medium-sized city of Vlastipol. He survived the war because he, along with his family, was sheltered in a barn on a farm owned by a client, Luther Bortsov. When the roundup of Jews became imminent, Bortsov offered the sanctuary of his property to the Potemkins. The punishment for harboring Jews was death, and many Christians died as a result. When a rumor spread that Bortsov was harboring Jews, two national policemen came onto the property with dogs, who began to sniff for fugitives in hiding places. When the police got within two thousand feet of the barn, Bortsov intercepted them and invited them to his farmhouse to try some liquor he had just made in a still on the property. After drinking and eating for much of the afternoon, the two policemen left. They would return twice more, but only to sample Bortsov's homemade spirits.

Before the war, Bortsov had been heavily indebted to Potemkin because of legal work necessitated by a soil runoff into a river that ran along the edge of the property. When the war ended, Potemkin forgave the debts and offered Bortsov free legal counsel for life, in gratitude for saving his family, which included his two young children, Rachel and Joshua.

Because Ugograd was a hugely diverse and culturally significant city, Potemkin knew it would afford him and his family opportunities unavailable in Vlastipol.

Amos Sephard was street smart and never harbored visions of idealism. He owned two taxicabs in Knenchin and hoped to build a fleet. When the war came, he changed his name to Sarov and got a government contract to chauffeur the Army's top military brass. As part of his ruse, he wore a highly polished gold crucifix, and he purposely kept his two top shirt buttons open so he could display it prominently. His features were plain and un-Semitic, and he was never suspected of being a Jew. At the war's end, the government gave him a civilian medal for his meritorious service. In a simple civil ceremony, the vice-president of the country hung the medal around his neck and then kissed him lightly on each cheek.

"The best hiding place," he said, "is right in front of them. They will never think to look there."

He knew there would be a greater opportunity to build a taxicab fleet in Ugograd than anywhere else in the country.

The migration had begun.

# Chapter VII

## Trying to Find God on the High Holidays

The phone began to ring in the apartment. As each Jewish migrant came to Ugograd to settle, they first called Sasha and Bushkin.

The new residents agreed to stay in touch with one another.

With the Jewish High Holidays, Rosh Hashanah and Yom Kippur, approaching, Bushkin and Sasha thought it would be appropriate to host a religious service in their apartment. Invitations were sent to Isadore and Yetta Samonovich, Tatyana Samuelson, Vasily Ginsberg, Yakov and Sarah Potemkin and children, and Amos Sephard.

Bushkin would act as the rabbi, although he acknowledged to Sasha that he was totally unprepared for such a role.

"Don't underestimate yourself," she told him. "Sometimes it is only when the outsider ascends to the 'stage' that perspective is restored."

"I hope you're right, Sasha."

"You know my father, a deeply religious man, was perpetually irritated with the rabbis," Sasha told him. "He thought that the rabbinate had become far too politically active and far less spiritual. After almost every sermon, he would become angry. He would say, 'The rabbi doesn't know what he's talking about. He has no idea of the real world. Why doesn't he stick to

43

religious interpretation and spiritualism instead of making statements about this group or that cause? Most of them have never been past the front door of life, yet they continue to offer social solutions that are profoundly naive, baseless and stupid.' My mother would say to him, 'Daniel, if it makes you angry to go, why do you go?'

"'That's what Jews do,' he answered. 'They go to the synagogue and listen to the rabbi.' Then he would leave the room in anger. My mother would just shake her head."

"Oh, so you're like your father," laughed Bushkin. "And that's where you get that temper!"

"Shut up," Sasha said, as she echoed Bushkin's laughter.

Bushkin next prepared for the service. He went to Ner Israel, the synagogue that was nearing its conversion to a gymnasium. With the help of some porters from his apartment building, he brought back fifty prayer books, three Torahs and a shofar.

As he reviewed the prayer book and Torah to prepare for the recitation of the service, he felt terribly awkward. How do you praise God during the Days of Awe when your people, the chosen, have been murdered almost to the point of extinction?

Nonetheless, he stood at 10 a.m. on the day of Rosh Hashanah at his dining room table as his guests sat in front of him on either dining room or living room chairs. There weren't enough people for a minyan.

As he went through the service, he recited the standard prayers. God was praised, extolled and revered. God was asked to grant peace and mercy. God was looked at as a source of peace. Bushkin asked God to restore Israel, though he felt terribly empty in making this request.

He recited the standard Hebrew prayers, including the Shema, Barechu, Shehecheyanu and Aleinu. He did the Kaddish and referred to the shofar.

He read from the Torah the story of Abraham and the sacrifice, the beginnings of Judaism.

Near the end of the service he gave a sermon. "This is a difficult time," he told his gathering.

"We are the few and maybe we are the faithful. Yet surely we are the skeptical.

"A year ago, none of us could have imagined being here. Yet we are here--in God's house--praising him, while, no doubt, feeling wronged and betrayed. It is only natural to feel this way.

"We met here this morning looking for meaning. I don't have many answers. A short while ago I met Sasha Liebowitz. I found her hiding in a mountain outside of Tashni. The next day in that city, we walked to the old Jewish section and came to a synagogue, Bnai Jacob.

"We went into the synagogue and found this Torah." At that point Bushkin removed the wrappings he made the day he found the scroll and held it up.

"As you can see, it is covered with red markings. This is blood. In some sense this is the ironic tie that binds us. On the one hand, the Torah, the five books of Moses, reflects the scholarship of our people--the ability of the ancient scribes to put our oral traditions in a literary form that has been handed down from generation to generation. On the other hand, the blood reflects another of our traditions, the effort of people to destroy us. This is a remarkably intolerable legacy.

Remarkable in that a minority can accomplish so much in law, medicine, business, science, literature, scholarship and religion, and yet remarkable still in that as a result of our ability we became the fodder for the mob. In once sense, we gave the heathens light, hope, goods, and scholarship. In another sense our ultimate repayment has been vilification and murder.

"This is extraordinary and it is wrong.

"Yet we are here today as Jews. We, the few, are survivors. No doubt from our seeds we will grow again. It is our destiny, ultimately, to again bring light into the world. But, God, please finally spare us from the mob. As we provide the light, let them never again destroy us. God, we ask you that such darkness never be shed on us again."

Bushkin then paused and looked to the congregation and said, "Amen." They responded in unison--"Amen."

With that the service ended, although Bushkin intended to have a final benediction and to do Ein Keiloheinu.

At the conclusion of the service, the congregants embraced one another. Sasha kissed Bushkin lightly on the cheek. "I'm proud of you, darling," she told him.

As she showed the guests to the door, Vasily Ginsberg was the last to exit. He began to talk to Sasha outside the apartment, as Bushkin tidied up from the congregants. Ginsberg began to tell her that even though he had just come into town, he was busy with new enterprises. He was a brazen self-promoter and name-dropper.

He didn't so much talk to her as he talked down to her. Everything he said was done to impress her. Every sentence had an important name, dollar amount, or deal reference. The conversation was one sided, as if he was the teacher and she was the naive schoolgirl. And through it all, he turned on his charm. Though he was brazenly disingenuous and self-aggrandizing, his words had an attraction. She wanted to listen to him. He was the braggart who made you want to hear him brag. He was the illusionist who made you want to hear about his illusions. He was the promoter who made you want to hear about his promotions. She was beginning to be mesmerized by him. She was awe-struck. She showed him to the elevator. As she did, he said, "I hope to see more of you." She didn't answer.

As she returned to the apartment, she thought about his charm, the largesse of his ideas, and the importance of what he seemed to be saying and doing. She was impressed by him and star struck.

When she came back to the apartment, Bushkin asked where she had gone. "I walked Vasily Ginsberg to the elevator," she said.

"Oh," he replied, "he is pretty notorious."

She didn't reply.

"I will soon have to prepare for Yom Kippur," he told her, changing the subject.

One day when he was home late in the afternoon after teaching a class, he retrieved the phone messages. One was for Sasha from Vasily Ginsberg. When she came home early that evening, he gave her the message and she promptly returned the phone call.

"What did he want?" asked Bushkin.

"Oh, he wanted to talk to me."

"About what?"

"He just wanted to talk, that's all."

"Did he want anything else?" asked Bushkin.

"He asked me to have lunch with him."

"Are you going?"

"No," she replied, and Bushkin dropped the subject.

Yom Kippur arrived--the holiest of holy days--the Jewish Day of Atonement. The day Jews fasted and atoned for their sins. The day Jews bared their soul before God.

Bushkin began the service, during which he acknowledged sins against God. He recognized God's majesty, and then he broke off from the routine of the service.

"God," he said, "if we have sinned against You, then we ask You: Why have so many sinned against us? Have You sinned against us?

"We come before You to ask for forgiveness and to forgive our enemies. Yet our enemies have been many and our numbers few.

"It is hard for us to ask for forgiveness and to forgive. It is hard to be righteous, when our righteousness has been unrewarded.

"It is hard to look into our souls, when our souls are so few.

"Why God, oh why God, do we come before You to ask for forgiveness, when the sins have been against us?"

Bushkin then paused. "I'm not up to this on this day," he told his gathering. "I can't proceed. The words of asking for forgiveness have no meaning for me this day, the holiest of holy days. You will excuse me, please." With that Bushkin left the apartment, went outside and started to walk.

48

The guests soon followed, either saying nothing or saying they understood his feeling, as they felt similarly. Only Vasily Ginsberg stayed.

As Bushkin walked, trying to gather himself while coming to grips with his emotions, Ginsberg started to converse with Sasha.

"Are you serious about this guy, Bushkin?" he asked her.

"Yes."

"Do you love him?"

"I think so, Vasily."

"Do you think it is possible to love more than one?"

"Yes. You know," she continued, "I'm beginning to feel very awkward."

"Do you want to feel awkward, Sasha?"

"I don't know. Please go now. Let me wait for Levi to return. This has not been a good day. Please go."

"Good-bye," he said, and kissed her lightly on the cheek.

About an hour later, Bushkin returned.

"Where did you go?" Sasha asked.

"I just walked."

"Did you reconcile anything?"

"I'm not sure, Sasha. I'm sorry I disappointed the group, but I just wasn't up to this."

"I understand, Levi. You'll do better next time."

"Next time?" he responded. "After this time, I don't know if there will be a next time. I don't think I'm equipped for this. I'm a literature professor, not a rabbi."

Several days later, a letter arrived from Yakov Potemkin, the lawyer.

Dear Levi,

I want to thank you and Sasha for hosting us on the High Holidays.

I completely understood your reaction on Yom Kippur. Perhaps inadvertently you expressed the legitimate feelings of the group.

These are difficult times, as we have been uprooted and have been forced to resettle. We are all going through a difficult time of personal questioning and reexamination.

However, the fact that you and Sasha so magnanimously hosted the group on the High Holidays may be a start to redeveloping a Jewish community in Ugograd.

As you are well aware, the city has numerous abandoned synagogues. I feel if we contact the city, I'm sure we could get the deed to one of the buildings. By doing this, it would help us establish a greater Jewish identity in Ugograd, and we would attract more co-religionists. On the other hand, such an effort would enhance our visibility and may attract the visceral reaction of the community's anti-Semites.

In any event, I look forward to discussing this and other important matters with you in the near future.

With kindest regards,
Yakov Potemkin, Esquire

# Chapter VIII

## Shul, Sasha and Shylock

A letter arrived on the desk of Nikita Krichev, Head of Property Disposition, the City of Ugograd:

Dear Mr. Krichev,

As a member of the Ugograd Hebrew Congregation, I would like to discuss with you the possibility of the city deeding one of the synagogues now in its possession to our congregation for use as a religious sanctuary.

I trust you will be receptive to this request, and I look forward to discussing this matter with you at your earliest possible convenience.

Yours very truly,

Levi Bushkin, Acting Rabbi

A few days later, Bushkin's literary class finished its discussion of Shakespeare's The Merchant of Venice. At the conclusion of class, Bushkin issued the following assignment: "In two weeks a paper of not more than ten pages will be due on your interpretation of The Merchant of Venice. You will have great flexibility with this exercise in terms of your ability to interpret events and characters in a context which will include, but not be limited to, moral, religious, literary, business, and economic matters and issues. Particular emphasis should be given to the characters of Shylock,

51

Antonio, Jessica, Bassanio and Portia. Be creative, thoughtful and incisive, and give me your best effort. All assignments, without fail, must be in by the deadline."

The day he issued the assignment, a letter arrived from Nikita Krichev saying he would meet Bushkin to discuss the possibility of the city deeding a synagogue to the congregation. Bushkin called Krichev and set up a 3:30 p.m. appointment two days later, on a Thursday. He asked Yakov Potemkin, now the lawyer for the congregation, to accompany him. The two arrived precisely at 3:30 p.m. Krichev's assistant advised them that he would be with them shortly. At 3:50 p.m., Bushkin asked the assistant when they would be able to see Mr. Krichev. She went to his office to see him and returned an instant later. "He will be with you momentarily," she replied. At 4:15 p.m., Krichev still had not met Bushkin and Potemkin.

"Please ask him when he can meet us," said an irritated Bushkin. "We've been waiting forty-five minutes," he reminded her as she walked to his office. When she returned, the assistant told them impolitely, and, in their opinion, insincerely, that an emergency had occurred and Mr. Krichev could not see them, but he would be able to reschedule the appointment the following Thursday at 3:30 p.m. Both Bushkin and Potemkin felt that Krichev was being disingenuous, but agreed to a meeting a week later.

When Bushkin returned home that evening, he told Sasha about his experience with Krichev. Rather than answer him, she told him that Vasily Ginsberg had called her at work and wanted to have lunch with her.

"This is becoming a recurrent theme with him," he said.

"I know, Levi."

"What are you going to do?"

"I don't know."

"This is becoming awkward," he replied sharply.

"I know, Levi." Following her answer, the two let the subject drop.

The following Thursday, Bushkin and Potemkin again were at Krichev's office at 3:30 p.m., the agreed-upon time. Bushkin reminded the assistant about what happened previously. The assistant looked at him contemptuously.

At 4 p.m. Bushkin and Potemkin still waited.

Bushkin now approached the assistant and told her very acidly that if "Mr. Krichev does not meet us in the next five minutes, we are leaving."

At 4:05 p.m., the two left without saying a word.

When Bushkin returned home, he called Father Yosef Vagins, a leading theologian whom Bushkin met with briefly when he came to Ugograd, immediately following the end of the war. Bushkin explained to Vagins that with a small settlement of Jews in Ugograd, a congregation had formed and the group was looking to obtain a deed of one of the many synagogues now in the city's possession. Bushkin and Father Vagins agreed to meet the next day, Friday.

When Bushkin arrived, Vagins saw him immediately and greeted him warmly. "How is my Jewish friend?" Vagins asked as Bushkin came into his office.

"Fine," he replied.

"Sit down," returned Vagins, "and make yourself comfortable."

"You know why I'm here. Can you help us?"

"I think so. You know, when you obtain your synagogue, your visibility will be heightened. Be aware of the anti-Semites."

"How do you know we will get the building, Father?"

"I have already taken care of it. Call Krichev's office on Monday."

"Krichev won't even see me."

"Call the office on Monday," repeated Vagins. As Bushkin stood up and was prepared to leave the office, he thanked Vagins profusely for his help.

"Don't be a stranger," said Vagins. "I'm here to help you. Good Shabbos."

"Thank you," said Bushkin. "I appreciate that." With that he left the office.

Following Vagin's instructions, he called Krichev's office on Monday. Krichev's assistant answered the phone. Recognizing Bushkin's voice, she said, "Dr. Bushkin, how are you?"

"Fine."

"What time will you be over?"

"Three-thirty."

"We will be here waiting for you."

"Okay," he said as he hung up.

When Bushkin arrived at 3:30 p.m., Krichev's assistant smiled at him warmly. "Dr. Bushkin, it's so good to see you again. How are things going at the University?"

"Fine."

"I am so sorry about the previous confusion, but problems arose that couldn't be helped."

"I'm sure," replied Bushkin.

"In this envelope is the deed to one of our synagogues, Brith Shalom. It is one of our smaller ones. However, if you outgrow it, I'm sure we will be in a position to give you a larger building."

"I am sure you will," said Bushkin with a trace of amusement in his voice.

"Thank you," Bushkin told her and left the building.

As Bushkin left the office, Krichev's assistant walked back to his office.

"Did you give the Jew the deed?" he wanted to know.

"Yes."

"Good," he replied. "I hope the synagogue burns with them, and the Jew-lover, Father Vagins, in it."

At that point, Krichev's assistant left the office.

Krichev immediately called Andrei Traicov of the anti-Semitic National Organization (NO).

"I gave the Jew the deed to the synagogue," Krichev told Traicov.

"You know what that means," said Traicov.

"What?" responded Krichev.

"There will be more Jews in Ugograd," he said as he hung up the phone.

When Bushkin returned home that evening, he advised Sasha that the congregation had received the deed to a synagogue.

"I wonder if we are becoming too visible," she said.

"That's always a risk, Sasha. That's always a risk."

He then excused himself and began to review the interpretive papers on <u>The Merchant of Venice</u>, which were due that day.

He turned to Tito Malenkov's paper first. Malenkov, an economics major and a literature minor, had impressed Bushkin during class discussions with his absorbing intellect and by his ability to synthesize multiple concepts into a cogent, related and singular analysis.

Bushkin began his paper with eager anticipation, and he wasn't disappointed.

Malenkov wrote:

Shylock is the focal point of the play. In <u>The Merchant of Venice</u>, he is the money-lender, the Jewish usurer.

Yet the world of commerce needs money and lenders. In reality, it couldn't function efficiently without them. Since the charging of interest was forbidden by the Church in the Middle Ages, it became an occupation opened to the Jews, who were not permitted, by law, to enter most other fields. To be sure, money is the lender's capital and interest is the payment for its use. Businessmen seek to preserve and grow their capital and receive the highest return for it. This is the essence of commerce and appropriate self-interest.

However, at a time when there were very few Jews in England (the Jews had been expelled late in the 13th century and weren't readmitted until 1653, approximately a half century after the play was written), Shakespeare sets the play in Venice, a leading commercial center. In 1175, some one hundred and fifteen years prior to the expulsion, the Jews were providing at least a quarter of the yearly income to the Crown. To protect this source of taxation, the Crown permitted only the Jews to be serious money-lenders.

In Venice, similarly, the Jews were money-lenders. They were pawnbrokers (poor-people's banks). They lived in a ghetto in the city. The right to operate the banks was done by a "condotta," which was revoked in 1396. In Venice, the Jews could not participate freely in all mercantile activities.

In <u>The Merchant of Venice</u>, Shakespeare depicts Shylock as miserly and cunning, a perfect foil for the kindly and generous Antonio. Shylock hates Antonio. "I'll hate him," he says, "for he is a Christian." His dislike for Antonio also stems from the fact that when he makes a loan, he does not charge interest. He has also lent money to Shylock's borrowers so they can avoid foreclosure.

Shakespeare has carefully and unequivocally contrasted two of the play's leading characters, the affable Christian Antonio and the ruthless Jew, Shylock.

Shylock, however, is more than a money-lender. He is vengeful. He makes a loan of 3,000 ducats to Bassanio on the basis of Antonio's bond. Bassanio needs the money to woo Portia. Shylock foregoes his usual high interest rate. Instead if the money is not paid at the appointed time, he can cut off one pound of flesh from Antonio's body.

Adding to Shylock's depth of hatred is that his daughter and only child, Jessica, had eloped with Lorenzo, a Christian and a friend of Antonio. As a result of the elopement, Jessica becomes a Christian.

When she leaves her father's house, Jessica has taken much of his wealth. (Her journey from Shylock's house to the sunlight and freedom of Belmont is viewed symbolically as a journey from hatred to love and from sterility to fruition.)

"I would my daughter were dead at my foot, and the jewels in her ear! Would she were hearsed at my foot, and the ducats in her coffin!" Shylock says in reaction to these developments.

Shakespeare has now made it clear that Shylock's attack on Antonio will be total and to the extent allowed under the bond; indeed, if necessary, he will demand his pound of flesh.

Shylock's appetite for vengeance and money is contrasted with that of Portia's Christian lover, Bassanio. Under the terms of her father's will, her lover must choose from among three caskets: one of gold, silver and lead. The suitor who picks the correct casket, the one with Portia's picture in it, will win her.

Previous suitors, the Prince of Morocco and the Prince of Arragon, have chosen incorrectly, picking the gold and silver caskets, respectively.

Bassanio rejects the golden casket as a symbol of "outward shows." He also rejects the silver casket. He then chooses the casket of "meagre lead," the least attractive of the three. Portia is overwhelmed by the choice because she loves Bassanio. Bassanio is able to judge correctly because his motive is love, in contrast to Shylock, whose lust is for the material and who would have likely chosen the more valuable metals had he had the choice.

Subsequently, a letter arrives from Antonio. Bassanio opens it. None of Antonio's ships have returned safely and the loan can't be paid on time.

As the story unfolds, Antonio is allowed to leave jail in Venice. He hopes to receive mercy. Instead, Shylock refuses to be a "soft and dull-eyed fool."

"I will have my bond," Shylock says.

Antonio knows that Venice is a major trade center, and debt repayment cannot be minimized. He also knows the Duke of Venice must judge the case in accordance with the contract. Antonio is resigned to his fate. "He seeks my life," Antonio says.

The Duke of Venice feels Shylock should take "pity on his losses."

Shylock is adamant. Even when Bassanio offers 6,000 ducats (twice the amount of the loan), Shylock refuses.

The Duke of Venice asks Shylock a question: "How shalt thou hope for mercy, rendering none?"

Shylock cites the mistreatment of many Venetian slaves as a precedent for his treatment of Antonio, and says the pound of flesh is "dearly bought" and belongs to him.

Antonio is without hope. He tells Bassanio "to live still, and write mine epitaph."

Shylock whets the knife on the sole of his shoe.

The Duke welcomes Balthasar, who is Portia dressed like a Doctor of Laws. She asks Antonio if his bond is valid. He says it is. She says Shylock must be merciful.

Shylock is shocked. Portia tells Shylock mercy is an attribute of God. She points out that all people "pray for mercy" and "that same prayer" should teach us all to "render the deeds of mercy."

Portia says Venetian law is binding, and Shylock can collect his pound of flesh.

Shylock hails the wisdom of the young judge and calls him "noble," "excellent," "wise and upright."

Shylock produces a scale to weigh the pound of flesh.

Portia, however, warns Shylock that he may take a pound of flesh, but no more. He may not take a "jot of blood." She warns him "if one drop of Christian blood" is shed, Shylock's "land and goods" will be confiscated by "the state of Venice."

Shylock realizes he has been foiled. He will now take Bassanio's offer of three times the amount of the bond. Portia decides otherwise. Shylock will have "nothing but the penalty," "just a pound of flesh," no more, no less. If he takes even "in the estimation of a hair" more than a pound of flesh he will die and all his goods will be confiscated.

Realizing he has been foiled, Shylock asks for the amount of the bond. Bassanio offers it. Portia points out the court was witness to Shylock refusing the money. Therefore, he has in effect forfeited it. Portia reminds Shylock that the laws of Venice forbid an alien from directly or indirectly attempting to seek the life of a citizen.

She has evidence that he seeks Antonio's life. She commands him to beg the mercy of the Duke. The Duke pardons Shylock, sparing his life, but adds that the penalty for the state taking half of Shylock's goods will be reduced if he evidences some "humbleness."

Shylock is adamant at such a proposal: "Nay, take my life and all," he declares.

Following the Duke's merciful example, Antonio says he will take only half of Shylock's goods due him. Half of Shylock's goods are held in trust in order to give them to his son-in-law Lorenzo upon his death on two conditions: First the usurer must become a Christian; second he must deed everything to Jessica and Lorenzo. Shylock agrees to the settlement.

In essence, the high action of the comedic drama ends at that point. The play undeniably is fraught with anti-Semitic overtones.

Shylock is ruthless. The Christians are kind. Shylock is the usurer. The Christians are the beleaguered borrowers. The Christians are merciful. Shylock is merciless. (The Duke of Venice calls Shylock "an inhuman wretch, /Uncapable of pity.")

The play also tends to enforce a religious stereotype to those who harbor ill feelings towards the Jews. (As this paper has documented, the Jews in the Middle Ages were allowed to be money-lenders [usurers] when the law permitted them little other activity and the Church forbade the charging of interest.)

When the play ends, Shylock is a defeated man. He has lost his daughter, his possessions, and his religion. Still, this outcome played favorably to the Elizabethan audiences of Shakespeare's time. Since Shylock becomes a Christian, he is now capable of salvation, which, as a Jew, he would have been incapable of.

In a sense then, all's well that ends well. Still, one wonders how the comedic-drama would have played if the roles of the Christian borrower and the Jewish usurer had been reversed. No doubt, had they been, the humor would have given way to outrage.

As Bushkin finished the paper he said, "Sasha, come here, please. I want you to read this. I think you will find this interesting."

At that moment the phone rang. Bushkin answered it.

"Sasha, it's for you."

"Who is it?"

"It's Vasily Ginsberg, the world's smartest, richest man." As he handed her the phone, he looked at her warily and then abruptly left the room.

"Please stop calling me here," said Sasha, and then the two began to talk.

# Chapter IX

## Sasha and the Dedication

Bushkin was home. He had a late class that morning. The door bell rang. The porter brought in long-stemmed roses and a card. The card read:

Sasha,
After a long search, these were the most exquisite I could find; yet they are no match for your beauty.
Vasily Ginsberg

Bushkin read the card and reacted angrily. He called Sasha at the hospital.

"Your friend, Vasily Ginsberg, sent you roses and a card."

"Isn't that nice," she said.

"I don't think so, Sasha. You and I are going to have to discuss this tonight. Either he goes or I go," he said as he abruptly hung up.

That evening the two began a heated conversation.

"You have a choice to make," said Bushkin. "If you want to start seeing Mr. Ginsberg, I think it would be best if you move out."

"Don't tell me what to do," she said. "Maybe I'll start to see him and you'll move out. It is just as much my apartment as it is yours."

"Oh, is that so! Well, who pays the rent every month, and who signed the lease, Sasha. I don't want to sleep with you tonight. Take your stuff and go into the other room."

"This is my bedroom, too," she said.

At that point he pushed her into the hall and threw some sheets and pillows at her.

"I don't want to see you tonight," he yelled from inside the bedroom.

"You are being a real ass," she countered from the hall.

Neither slept well that evening. When they awoke the next morning, each refused to speak to the other.

That evening, each apologized, but the conversation soon became heated.

"Do you want to start seeing him?" Bushkin asked.

She didn't answer.

"I asked you: Do you want to start seeing him?"

She then abruptly left the room in tears.

"I think it's time we end it," he shouted. "If we end it now, there will be less hurt."

She then returned. "I don't want to end it," she said. "I love you."

"Well, if you love me, you'll tell Mr. Ginsberg to stop calling you."

"I don't know if I want to do that, Levi."

"You can't have it both ways. I need your decision."

She didn't say anything. The two soon went to bed, again sleeping in other rooms. When they awoke and saw each other the next morning, there was a deep tension. The compatibility they had shared since they had met in the mountains outside of Tashni had evaporated. It had given way to a deep anxiousness and a developing mistrust.

"Have you decided what you want to do?" he asked.

"I can't, Levi."

"You better. I can't be intimate with you while you date him."

"I am not good with ultimatums," she said. "Not yet, anyway."

"What do you see in him?" Bushkin asked. "I know, Sasha, it's his manner, and the wealth he flaunts. You are infatuated with a facade, not a person. You are infatuated with an image. You are a fool. If you end up with him, you'll get hurt."

"How do you know?"

"Because he hurts everyone: his investors, his partners, his wives. He's destructive and hurtful. If you end up with him, you'll soon wonder what happened and what you saw in him."

"People can change," she said.

"The weather can change from day to day, but the pattern remains the same. What makes you think the pattern will be different? Ingrained behavior is the hardest thing to change. If you buy into him, you will be left with nothing but heartache. For such a smart girl, you sure do have your blind spots."

"Who are you to criticize me. Since when are you so perfect?"

"I never said I was, Sasha. But I love you, not a facade. This is your problem, not mine."

"Why are you so sure of yourself, Levi?"

"This is one time I can see for the both of us."

"Don't be so sure of yourself," she replied.

"This is the easiest call I ever made, Sasha."

At that point, Sasha broke off the conversation.

"Let me sleep with you tonight," she said.

"Okay," he replied.

As they got into bed, she turned and held him tightly.

"I love you," she said.

"I love you, too," he replied.

The next morning she awoke first and began to anxiously pace the bedroom floor. In turn, the noise of her pacing woke him up.

"What's the problem, Sasha?"

"I'm so damn confused," she replied.

"If you're confused, I think it's better that we break it off."

"But I don't want to."

"If you want to go exploring with Mr. Ginsberg, I'm not going to hold you back."

"I want to stay with you, Levi. I'm going to write Vasily telling him to stop calling me."

"Are you sure you want to do that?"

"I'm sure."

"I love you, Sasha."

"I love you, too, Levi."

Before she left for work, she wrote the following note to Vasily Ginsberg:

Your attention and card were so flattering. However, I'm in a relationship and, for the moment, we can only be friends.

Sasha

When Bushkin returned home that evening, he asked her if she had written the note. She said she had.

"Is it over?" he asked.

"Yes, Levi."

"I hope so," he replied and let the subject drop.

"Sasha, how was your day at work?"

"Fine."

"You know we will have to convene the shul members," Bushkin said, "to discuss the administration, maintenance and funding of the synagogue. This is a big undertaking for such a small group."

"I can understand that, Levi."

"Please call everyone and set up a meeting a week from now."

"I will," she replied.

The group, including Vasily Ginsberg, convened. Sasha felt awkward with him there, as did Bushkin.

Bushkin opened the meeting by saying, "The synagogue will be costly to maintain. We will have maintenance and utility bills, and we may need to hire a security guard. We will have to depend on this small group to fund the costs. We will need donations from each of you."

Bushkin then went around the table and asked each person what he or she was capable of giving. Sasha agreed to a week's pay, as did Bushkin. Isadore Samonovich, who had leased the Sandler's Department Store property, agreed to donate twenty-five percent of his Christmas Eve's gross sales. Tatyana Samuelson, the artist, said she would give the entire proceeds from her first sale. Yakov Potemkin, the lawyer, said he would donate a week's pay. Amos Sephard, owner of a small cab company, said he would donate a week's gross revenue. After hearing the pledges, Vasily Ginsberg paused and then with a haughty, almost disdainful laugh, said, "Whatever the highest donation is, I will give 50 percent more." As he made his pledge, he made eye contact with Sasha, as he had done often that evening. She, however, avoided eye contact with him.

Bushkin thanked the group for its magnanimity. He said he would continue to act as a rabbi but hoped a replacement could be found in a year. "As to services," he said, "it might be suitable if we can hold them twice a month, on a Friday night or Saturday morning, and on the first day of Rosh Hashanah and on Yom Kippur. During weekend services we will acknowledge the other holidays, celebrations and festivals as they immediately approach, and we will give attention to Simchat Torah, Sukkot, Chanukah, Shavuot, Purim, Passover, and Tisha B'Ab. On the first night of Passover, we can hold a Seder at the synagogue."

"That's a reasonable approach," voiced Yakov Potemkin. The group concurred.

"Now that we have the synagogue, I'm sure we will receive additional publicity and hopefully we can attract more residents who can give us numerical strength and ease our financial burdens," Bushkin said.

As the formal business of the meeting concluded, and the guests were having coffee and dessert, Yakov Potemkin approached Bushkin, who was alone in the kitchen and was about to bring additional pastries to his guests in the dining room.

"I'll bet," Potemkin said, "Vasily Ginsberg never contributes a nickel to the maintenance of the shul. It's always the ones who advertise themselves the loudest who never give a cent." Bushkin smiled at Potemkin agreeably, but didn't reply.

The meeting soon adjourned. As the guests exited the apartment, Bushkin said to Sasha, "I didn't like the way Vasily Ginsberg stared at you this evening."

"I didn't notice," she said as she walked away from him into another room, avoiding an argument that she knew would come if she gave him a direct answer.

Unknown to Bushkin, Ugograd's mayor, Joseph Gromyko, planned a photo session and a ceremony on the day the synagogue would be officially turned over to the Ugograd Hebrew Congregation.

Bushkin was advised by mail of the dedication ceremony, and he and Yakov Potemkin represented the congregation at the event. Bushkin asked other members to attend, but with the exception of Sarah Potemkin and Yetta Samonovich, no one else could be present.

While those who couldn't attend politely called or told him they could not make it due to the press of other matters, he received a terse note from Vasily Ginsberg: "I would consider being there but, of course, urgent and important business matters will not allow me the time for such an activity."

Bushkin read the note and threw it away. "Who is this guy kidding?" Bushkin thought to himself. "I know if Sasha had invited him and had agreed to meet him there, he would have attended."

Bushkin found each time he had the most minimal contact with Ginsberg, he became irritated and his mood bordered on rage.

The ceremony took place on a Wednesday afternoon. It was a lovely fall day in early November. The air had a refreshing crispness, and an ever-present breeze made a collage of foliage sway lightly in the trees.

As the ceremony began, Mayor Gromyko, from the top step of the synagogue, said, "This is a day that the citizens of Ugograd should long remember, as we are doing a good deed.

"We are turning back a synagogue to its rightful owners, the Jews of Ugograd.

"We can never address the wrongs that were done to our Jewish citizens. However, this gesture, small as it is, will hopefully ensure the small Jewish community will grow. I can speak for all here when I say the Jews are welcomed in Ugograd."

A light applause followed.

The mayor next invited Bushkin to make some comments.

"We would like to thank the city for this gift, and we would also like to thank Father Yosef Vagins, whom I see standing off to my right. Father, please acknowledge yourself and wave to the crowd." He did so to polite applause. "Without Father Vagin's assistance," Bushkin went on, "I don't know if this day would have been possible."

Bushkin then continued his speech: "As citizens of Ugograd, we look forward only to the future. The past is part of our heritage which we can never forget; however, it is the future that we live for. We consider this synagogue part of the new beginning, and Ugograd is our home. Let's all live together in peace and harmony.

"Thank you all for coming."

Bushkin continued: "Now we will receive the keys from Mayor Gromyko, symbolic of the passing of ownership."

The mayor then presented the keys to Bushkin and Yakov Potemkin. Newspaper cameras clicked and TV cameras recorded the moment. Then Bushkin first, and Potemkin following, each embraced the mayor, who kissed each lightly on the cheek.

Following that exchange, Olga Tereshnova, a reporter from the <u>Informant</u>, asked Bushkin about his reactions to this day.

"We are elated," he said.

"Do you worry about anti-Semitism?" she queried.

"As Jews, we always worry about that."

She then asked Yakov Potemkin, "I understand Mr. Bushkin is your rabbi. What kind of spiritual leader is he?"

"Well, he is very spiritual, but he's a little rough," he said as he smiled at Bushkin.

"Thanks," Bushkin said mockingly while managing to return a smile at Potemkin.

"When the article and publicity circulate throughout the country," Tereshnova said, "do you hope more of your co-religionists will be attracted to Ugograd?"

"There is strength in numbers, but there is risk in visibility," he returned. "Listen, I hate to cut short this interview, but I have to return to the University to teach a class."

"Thank you for your time, Dr. Bushkin."

As the crowd dispersed, Father Vagins walked over to Andrei Traicov and Nikita Krichev, Head of Property Disposition, the City of Ugograd. Both, he knew, were members of the anti-Semitic National Organization (NO).

"You better not try anything," he said to the pair.

"I don't know what you're talking about," replied Traicov.

"Then keep me in ignorance," responded Vagins as he walked away.

The following day Tatyana Samuelson, now employed as a professor at the Art Institute, met with the president of the school. She explained to him that she had volunteered the payment from the next piece of artwork she sold toward the maintenance of the synagogue now in possession of the Ugograd Hebrew Congregation.

"I didn't know you acknowledged your Judaism," replied Savar Chernov, president of the school.

"I never denied it," she said. "I propose to do a sculpture of religions significance. I would like the school to buy it and donate it to the Ugograd Art Museum. In essence, through me, the purchase would represent a token of support to the Jews of Ugograd."

"I think we can go along with that," said Chernov. "Tell me, what should we pay?"

"Use your discretion," she said, "but be fair."

"We will, Tatyana."

As she got up to leave, she thanked him excessively for his cooperation. As she was about to walk through the door, he said to her, "Try not to make it too controversial."

She turned and said she wouldn't.

In turn, he rolled his eyes. He knew to expect otherwise.

# Chapter X

## Tatyana Samuelson's Expressionism

The table stood by a large window in her apartment. On it stood the clay, formless and in a mound. Her brain piqued her emotions. Her emotions taunted her senses.

Everything seemed to accelerate. Her thought processes elevated. First she stood; then she paced. She never experienced such a mood: Bitter over the message she wanted the clay to convey. Exhilarated over the prospect of the clay hardening and speaking out for her. As she continued to pace, Tatyana Samuelson never felt such a combination of rage and excitement before. Finally she was able to sit down. As she did, she began pounding the clay. Then her hands dug into the unformed mass as her fingers became an extension of her emotions. As she molded the clay, Samuelson thought about living in a sewer and coming out at night to forage for food. Her crime was that she was a Jew, although she didn't observe the faith. Because society said she was a Jew, it hunted her. She would never forgive society for trying to murder her.

She thought about having attended an impromptu service on Rosh Hashanah, where Levi Bushkin officiated. She felt spiritual that day, like never before. She also remembered Bushkin walking out on Yom Kippur. She empathized with him. Why should he ask

God for forgiveness, when a whole religion had been murdered to the point of near extinction?

As she sculpted the clay, she thought how society referred to her as a Jew-artist. She ignored the taunt. She knew that if society would not let her forget who she was, she would no longer need to be reminded. Her artistic expressionism would be society's reminder.

If society forced her to feel Jewish, she would let it know how a Jew felt.

The sculpture began to shape. She sculpted a Star of David. Around it she made a cross and attached it to the Star's upper horizontal points. At the point of attachment, the cross bent the Star's points, and it buckled it almost at its middle. She had created the impression that the cross was strangling the Star, and suffocating and murdering it. She painted the Star a pristine white. She sculpted small mound-like areas on the Star, some of which protruded from it and others hung below its linear elements. She painted the mound-like areas a deep, angry red to represent blood, and made the cross a midnight, moonless black.

She called her work "Religious Murder."

The piece was a symmetrical three feet high by three feet wide. She invited Savar Chernov, president of the Art Institute, to see it. He looked at it and then looked at her. "We have problems," he said.

"I know," she replied.

"Let's talk about this," he said.

"Okay," she answered.

The two went to a coffee shop that was on the street level and had outdoor seating. They sat outside.

"The museum will never accept this piece," Chernov told her.

"My art is my expression, my message," she replied. "Think of 'Religious Murder' as Tatyana Samuelson's 'Guernica.'"

"I understand your message," he said, "but this is Ugograd. The crime was there but not the outrage."

"How about my outrage?" Samuelson said. "Can't I express it?"

"You can, but not too loudly. Let me talk to my Board of Regents," he said as he politely excused himself.

At the meeting he said to the assembled regents, "Tatyana Samuelson, a graduate, as you know, of the Art Institute and a survivor of the Jewish extermination, came to me with the idea of a project which the school could purchase and then donate to the Ugograd Art Museum. The proceeds from the work would be given to the newly formed Ugograd Hebrew Congregation and would be used for the maintenance of its synagogue."

"How much did she get you for?" chimed Ivan Demonavitch, head of the Utility Company of Ugograd.

"She let me determine the price," responded Chernov, "but asked that it be a fair one."

"Isn't that rare for a Hebrew?" remarked Demonavitch.

"Shut up," warned Chernov.

"I'm sorry," said Demonavitch. "So what's the problem?" he asked.

"The problem," responded Chernov, "is the message."

"What is it?" asked Reza Trapov, a regent and head of the Ugograd Red Cross.

Chernov then had a porter bring in the work. He placed it on the middle of the large, spherical conference table. The group gathered en masse at the end of the table and studied the sculpture.

"This is an outrage," said Nicoli Shmelkov, president of the First National Bank of Ugograd.

"We can't approve anything like this," said Sophia Ruselana, president of the Public Employees Union.

"I agree," echoed Ivan Demonavitch.

"I have an idea," said Chernov. "Let me talk to Ms. Samuelson, and we will defer action until the next meeting."

"Listen," Nicoli Shmelkov told him, "if I were you, I wouldn't stir up controversy over some Jew and her art. If you create a storm of resentment, you may find yourself out of a position. The last time I looked, there weren't too many comparable positions for unemployed presidents of art colleges.

"You've got it pretty good here," he continued. "You have a good salary, a comfortable pension, and other excellent benefits, including a house.

"I would be prudent about this if I were you."

A week later Chernov met with Samuelson in his office at the Art Institute. "The regents," he said, "were unreceptive over the school buying the sculpture and donating it to the Ugograd Art Museum."

"I am not surprised," Samuelson said.

"I have a plan," he said. "But before I tell you, please get up and close the door. I don't want anyone to hear this."

"Okay," responded Samuelson.

"Come a little closer," he said. "I don't want to speak too loudly so someone can overhear us."

"Okay."

"Here is what I propose: The school will buy the sculpture and create a section in the lobby of the Main Administration Building called Expressionistic Art. Your sculpture will be on permanent exhibit with those of other avant-garde artists. Once a year, say for a two-week period, the exhibit will be lent to the Ugograd Art Museum. Also, the possibility exists that the exhibit will be in demand nationally and around the world. By doing it this way, the piece won't stand out. Instead, it will be an expression among other expressionism. Hence, the message, though poignant, will be softened. And who knows, one day when society confronts its genocide, maybe the piece can stand alone."

"I can live with that," replied Samuelson.

"Good. I will bring it up at the next Board of Regents meeting."

"Artistic freedom lives, somewhat," said Samuelson matter-of-factly.

"You're proof of that," responded Chernov. "I will let you know the outcome following the next meeting."

Samuelson departed Chernov's office.

Samuelson's sculpture was the first order of business at the meeting. "We have a chance, through a graduate and professor of this school, to address an horrific wrong. We have an opportunity, through her sculpture, to use art as a medium for which it was long intended--to commemorate evil and to be civilization's conscience," Chernov said.

"Ms. Samuelson has sculpted with brilliant artistry and with profound meaning. I'm enamored of her effort and hopefully I speak for the school when I say I'm proud to be associated with her and her art.

"I have discussed a plan with her that would make her work appear less controversial."

"What's the plan?" asked one of the regents.

"I've put the plan in writing. My assistant will pass it out now. Take a minute to read and digest it. Then we can discuss it."

After a pause, Ivan Demonavitch said, "I think I can go for this."

"Me too," chimed Sophia Ruselana.

"Is there any discussion?" said Chernov.

"No, except I think you're sticking your neck out," said Nicoli Shmelkov.

"Any more comments?" said Chernov.

There was silence.

"Let's have a vote," he said. "All in favor raise your right hand. All who disapprove raise your left hand. The motion carries five to two.

"Do the dissenters want to be noted in the minutes?"

Both said yes.

"Please note," he told his assistant, "that the nay votes were cast by Mr. Shmelkov and Ms. Ruselana."

A month later a $5,000 check arrived addressed to the Ugograd Hebrew Congregation c/o Levi Bushkin.

Bushkin immediately called Samuelson in her apartment.

"We got a check from the school. It was very considerate. Do you know how much was sent?"

"No," she replied, "and please don't tell me."

"Okay," he said. "Tell me how you feel with everything you've been through."

"Jewish," she said.

"How does that feel?"

"Very Jewish," Samuelson replied.

# Chapter XI

## Sasha's Dilemma

The squealing brakes could be heard for blocks. Then came the crash, metal on metal. Then there was a momentary silence. Then screaming. The crowd rushed over. An ambulance soon followed.

The collision of the cars had been head-on. The driver of the black car was dead. The passenger had to be removed. It seemed like his body was broken. He was laid on the sidewalk.

The ambulance arrived and he was placed in it. He was taken to University Hospital.

The injuries were multiple. The passenger was in shock. He had suffered a fractured pelvis, shoulder and rib. Sasha Liebowitz read the report. She recognized the name of the injured man. He was Alexander Shukov. Before the war, he was one of the country's leading anti-Semitic leaders. She remembered his anti-Jewish diatribes on radio and TV that were carried worldwide. Among other things, he said the Jews were responsible for the bubonic plague of the Middle Ages, and that Passover Matzos were made from the blood of Christian children whom Jews had murdered. He had helped poison the world's atmosphere against the faith. During the war, he was a high-ranking administrator in a death camp.

As she examined the patient, Sasha noted his blood count had dropped, indicating a ruptured spleen. She now knew if she didn't operate he would hemorrhage to death. His life and death would now rest with her. How ironic, she felt. How strange. What would he have done in a similar case? She had no doubt: He was a religious murderer, a Jew killer.

But she was a doctor, a healer. Her ethics demanded she save him. But who would know if he died what the reason would be.

She pondered her dilemma: should she try to save or kill him? She knew she would have to operate within forty-eight hours, or he would hemorrhage to death.

At home that evening she wasn't the same. Her manner was tense. Her eyes were opened so wide, she appeared to have been permanently startled. Her body was taut and rigid. She even breathed irregularly.

As she was having dinner with Bushkin, she cut her food but didn't eat it. As she sat there, Bushkin said to Sasha, "What's wrong?"

"Nothing," she snapped.

"Nobody acts like you're acting if nothing is wrong. Is it Vasily Ginsberg?"

"I wish it were that simple," she said.

"Why can't you tell me?"

"If I do," she said, "and something happens you may be implicated even though you had nothing to do with it."

"You're acting and sounding so strange."

"I know, Levi. In a couple of days, things will be a lot clearer. But I can't talk now. I'm going to bed."

"So early."

"Only if I can fall asleep. If not, I'll lay there and try to rest."

"I'm going to take a walk," said Bushkin. "I'll be in later. I'm here for you if you want to talk to me. I love you."

"I love you too, Levi."

She turned the lights off, laid rigidly on her back, and, unable to close her eyes, stared at the ceiling. He returned about 9 p.m. and walked into the room. He turned the lights on; her position had not changed.

"What's the matter?" he asked.

"I still can't say, Levi."

"I'm going to bed," he replied.

As she lay in bed, she weighed her options. Her family had been murdered by the likes of Shukov. Sasha now felt she was entitled to retribution. Her conscience interrupted. Daniel, her father, always had an expression: "Jews don't act that way." But he was dead, killed by a Shukov. What would he say if he were here? She heard the voice again: "Jews don't act that way. The Jews are the people of the Torah and Moses' law, the Ten Commandments."

But she asked Daniel's voice, "Didn't Menachem Begin blow up the King David Hotel, killing innocent people?"

"That was for Israel's independence," the voice answered.

"If the roles were reversed, what would Shukov do?" she asked.

"Jews don't act that way," the voice repeated. "Don't make me ashamed of you. Don't bring shame to your family."

She just lay there: thinking, contemplating, confused, angry, and a little afraid of herself. She closed her eyes and then opened them. Two a.m. came, then three, four, five and six. The alarm sounded.

She hadn't gotten any sleep, but she wasn't tired.

She knew she was running on nervous energy and adrenaline. With the sounding of the alarm, she jumped out of bed and showered.

Bushkin remained asleep.

After showering, she woke Bushkin up. "Hold me," she told him as she got into bed with him. He put his arm around her waist and squeezed her firmly and lovingly.

"Don't let me go," she said.

They held the embrace for ten minutes.

"I have to get dressed now," she said. "I'm going to the hospital early. I may have a surgery scheduled this afternoon."

"Is that what's bothering you, Sasha?"

"Not really. I'll be able to discuss this with you more fully in a few days."

She dressed quickly, skipped breakfast and walked to work.

She kept hearing her father's voice: "Jews don't act that way." And it repeated: "Don't bring shame to your family."

She still was confused.

At the hospital, she scheduled Shukov's surgery at 3 p.m. At the moment of the surgery, her medical instincts and training took over. He was no longer Shukov the anti-Semitic killer. He was her patient. Murder was no longer an option. She began to save him.

During the two hours of surgery, she repaired the lacerated areas of the spleen and stopped the hemorrhaging. She had saved Shukov's life.

Following surgery, she went to her office. She was emotionally distraught. The surgery left her tired and mentally drained. The previous day of probing her psyche left her in a disequilibrium to the point that she could barely move. She reclined in her chair and stared blankly at the far wall.

Finally she left the office and went home. She walked in at 9 p.m.

"I was worried about you," Bushkin said. "I tried calling the office several times, but the recording was on."

"I am all right, Levi."

"Can you talk to me?" he asked.

"Not now, Levi."

"You are making me upset, Sasha. What's wrong?"

"Give me a couple of days," she answered.

"Have it your way," he replied.

Several days later, Shukov's mother, Svetlana, and his wife, Mary, came to Sasha's office to thank her. At the entrance they saw a Mezuzah. They felt uneasy.

They walked in and told her assistant the purpose of the visit. The assistant walked back to Sasha's office and advised her of her visitors and the reason they wanted to see her.

Sasha refused to see them, and they understood why. Several days later, a letter arrived from Mary Shukov.

Dear Dr. Liebowitz,

I would like to thank you for your outstanding work and for saving my husband, Alexander.

Sincerely,

Mary Shukov

Liebowitz wrote back:

Dear Mrs. Shukov,

I tried to save him because, at heart, I am a healer, a humanist and a Jew.

I had it in my power to let him die, but I couldn't do it. When he lay before me wounded and powerless, my soul said save him.

Yet I know had the roles been reversed, he would have murdered me. Alexander Shukov and his ilk killed my family and my fiance. To him they weren't people, not flesh and blood, but faceless, numbered Jews who had to be exterminated.

Ultimately, however, it was I who saw a murderer as a human being who had to be saved, and I would do it again.

How ironic and how sad the religious murderer, the Jew killer, lives, and the civilized, because of their religion, died.

To me it is intolerable that the wrong person lives, saved by an individual whom your husband would have killed had he had the opportunity. And how ironic is it that he may yet murder me, his Jewish savior.

Sasha Liebowitz, M.D.

Mary Shukov, upon reading the letter, filed a complaint with the hospital against Dr. Liebowitz. Eventually the complaint was referred to the hospital president, I. F. Zaporkin. He read it and requested a meeting with Sasha.

"Did you write this?" he asked Dr. Liebowitz.

"Yes," she replied.

"I'm going to have to suspend you," Zaporkin said, "pending an administrative hearing by your peers. You are being suspended for conduct unbecoming a medical professional, which is strictly prohibited under our bylaws, and is cause for termination. Couldn't you have been more discreet? I don't want to do this. You're very capable, but pressures around here are such that you have left me no choice."

She left Zaporkin's office and went home. Yet she felt no regret for writing the letter.

She explained the entire situation to Bushkin. He comforted her.

"Would you have changed anything?" he asked.

"No," she replied.

"I'm here for you no matter what the outcome. I love you and I'll support you," he said.

"That was so sweet, Levi. I love you so very much."

Sasha was soon sent a notice that a hearing would convene three weeks from the date of the suspension. Bushkin asked if she wanted to discuss the matter with Yakov Potemkin, the lawyer. She said she didn't want to. He asked her to reconsider. She still declined.

Bushkin said he would have members of the Jewish community there for emotional support. Sasha said this would be helpful and was permitted under the hospital bylaws. When the hearing convened, fifteen were present, including Amos Sephard, proprietor of a small cab company; Isadore Samonovich, the owner of

Sandler's Department Store; and several others who had recently moved to Ugograd. Bushkin was so transfixed by the upcoming hearing, he didn't notice Vasily Ginsberg enter the room. Included among the other observers was Olga Tereshnova, a reporter for the Informant.

She was asked to leave by Zaporkin. He explained to her this wasn't a public meeting, but she would be advised of the outcome as soon as a decision had been rendered. She accepted the explanation without protest and left the meeting.

At the onset of the hearing, Dr. Liebowitz was advised that in the event of an unfavorable outcome, she could appeal the decision to the courts. She said she understood.

Zaporkin opened the hearing by saying Dr. Liebowitz had been placed on administrative leave because of "conduct unbecoming a medical professional and a member of University Hospital." Zaporkin told Dr. Liebowitz's colleagues that "the penalty for an unfavorable finding" by them "could range from a censure, fine, or temporary suspension, to an outright termination." He mentioned to the group that Dr. Liebowitz, prior to this time, "had compiled an enviable record in terms of being a team player, capable surgeon, and an asset to the hospital." He asked them to reread the letter she had written to Mary Shukov. They did.

Zaporkin asked her to explain herself.

She said, "How would you have reacted if you were in my predicament?"

No one answered.

Zaporkin asked if she had anything else to say.

"Yes," she replied.

"Go ahead," he told her.

"I saved him, didn't I? He's alive, isn't he? I hate what he stands for: intolerance, bigotry, and murder. He's an emotionally sick human being. I can't imagine you here condone what he is.

"Meanwhile, as a result of the anti-Semitism he stands for, I no longer have a family.

"Yet, tomorrow, if the situation presented itself, I would do my utmost to save him, but in some way I would hate myself for doing so.

"His deeds go unpunished. My act of humanity results in a hearing and possible dismissal. Had he died as a result of the surgery, we wouldn't be here. In a way, we're only here because he lived. What's on trial is only my attitude . . . my competence . . . and my unrepentant honesty."

After a pause, Zaporkin asked if any of the committee had any further questions. The members had none. Zaporkin asked if the group wanted time to deliberate or were the members ready to make a decision. The panelists talked briefly among themselves and advised Zaporkin they had reached a verdict.

He then asked each member to state his decision. The first four said Dr. Liebowitz should be reinstated immediately without any loss in pay or benefits. Dr. Modest Menchev, the fifth member of the group, abstained from voting, saying he's protesting why a hearing was necessary, given what Dr. Liebowitz has been through.

Sasha was elated at the outcome, as was Bushkin. When the decision was fully rendered, Vasily Ginsberg was the first to congratulate Sasha. He did so, embracing Sasha and kissing her lightly on the cheek. Bushkin was irritated at the gesture, but tried his best to mask his anger. He followed Ginsberg, embraced Sasha, and kissed her lightly on the lips. After doing so, he smiled lovingly at her. She returned the smile.

As the doctors exited the hearing, Zaporkin said to Dr. Menchev, "The next time someone from the 'nut fringe' needs surgery, please refer him to someone else."

"That may be kind of difficult," replied Dr. Menchev.

# Chapter XII

## Growth and Wanderlust

The large manila envelope arrived on Amos Sephard's desk, which was in the corner of a small garage where he kept his two cabs.

He opened it and read its contents carefully. Because of the death of its owner, the assets of the City Cab Company were being put up for sale. Ten taxicab licenses were being offered along with twelve vehicles and a five-car garage with a small office and a yard. Immediately Sephard called Feodor Pavlov, the business broker handling the sale.

"Why does Mrs. Netsov want to sell?" he asked.

"Since her husband died," Pavlov said, "she is having trouble managing the business and it's affecting her health. Her children don't want the business, and she is being advised to sell."

"Please forward me the last three years of profit and loss statements," he told Pavlov.

"You will have them before the day is out," he replied.

"Good, I will be driving the rest of the morning through the afternoon. I will review them upon my return, later today."

At 4 p.m., Sephard returned to the garage and the financial statements were on his desk. He reviewed them intently.

He felt the purchase price of $1,500,000 was high, but if he could renegotiate the price down and obtain favorable financing, the transaction could make sense and give him a credible presence in the marketplace.

He called Pavlov later that afternoon and arranged to meet him the next day. At that time, the two began discussing the acquisition.

"What's the best purchase price I can get?" he asked Pavlov.

"Probably $1,200,000," he was told.

"Do you think she would go for a $1,000,000?" Sephard countered.

"No," Pavlov said, "but you can try."

"Will she hold financing?" Sephard asked.

"You are better off if you discount the price, to try to arrange your own financing. She is more inclined to accept a lower offer if it is an all-cash transaction."

"Are there any banks that would finance this transaction?" asked Sephard.

"I think so," said Pavlov.

"Give me a couple of days to think about this, and I will call you with an offer."

"There are other cab companies looking at this transaction," Pavlov advised him.

"I am sure that's the case," Sephard said, "but I have to be prudent." With that exchange, the meeting ended.

For the next two days, Sephard reviewed figures and made various assumptions. He then called Pavlov and arranged a meeting the next day.

At the meeting, he said: "I will offer her $1,200,000 cash, but I'm going to have to finance one hundred percent of the purchase price. With only two cabs, I have very little cash. On the other hand, if I can get a bank loan for $1,200,000, I can pay it off in seven years at 10 percent interest and would have cash available for vehicle upkeep and replacement, given normal business conditions.

"I have spoken to my attorney, and he said if the offer is acceptable, he would draw up a contract with a 60-day financing contingency and settlement in 30 days."

"I will speak to Mrs. Netsov," said Pavlov.

A week later, Pavlov called Sephard to tell him the offer had been accepted and for him to draw up a contract.

"I will have my lawyer write the contract," Sephard said. "In the meantime, please suggest some banks I can contact for financing."

"I will," Pavlov replied.

A week later the contract was presented to Mrs. Netsov for signature.

She reviewed it with her attorney and signed it. Sephard was now under pressure to meet the sixty-day financing deadline.

Pavlov told Sephard about financing sources, and he advised him there were three banks whom he felt would look favorably on the transaction: the First National Bank of Ugograd, City Bank, and Fidelity United Bank. Sephard, with the assistance of his attorney, Yakov Potemkin, prepared a financing package and forwarded one to the head of the commercial loan department of each bank.

Potemkin suggested he might ask Vasily Ginsberg for assistance in arranging a loan. Sephard declined, saying he was "skeptical of having any dealings with him."

Within two weeks of the submission of the package, each bank denied him financing, unwilling even to discuss the matter.

At that point, Sephard called Pavlov as to a possible explanation of the refusals.

"Don't you know?" he asked Sephard.

"No doubt because of my religion," he said.

"That's right," answered Pavlov. "The big banks like dealing with blue bloods. They don't care if they make bad loans, so long as they are made with the right kind of people."

"What would you suggest now?" he asked Pavlov.

"There is a smaller bank south of the city called Fraternity Bank. You should send the loan submission directly to the bank president, M. N. Zagrev. I know Mr. Zagrev and I will alert him that it is coming."

Zagrev received the financing package and arranged to meet Sephard at his cab company. The two then visited City Cab and stayed on the premises to review the financial statements and Sephard's assumptions.

Zagrev questioned Sephard intensely and was satisfied with his answers.

"Before I give you an indication, I have a question to ask you."

"What's that?" said Sephard.

"Is it true you changed your name during the war and received a government contract to chauffeur the Army's top military brass?"

"Yes," he replied.

"Is it also true you were given a medal for meritorious service from the vice-president of the country?"

"Yes," he said, again.

"Look, even though we seldom finance one hundred percent of the acquisition price, we will probably make an exception here. I will recommend to our board of directors that it approve the loan.

"Anybody who did what you did to survive the war will somehow make a go of the acquisition and repay the loan."

"Thank you, sir," said Sephard.

"You will hear from us in two weeks," said Zagrev.

An excited Sephard called Yakov Potemkin with the news. "The president of Fraternity Bank said he will probably make the loan," he told him.

"Aren't you glad," Potemkin said, "you didn't listen to me and approach Vasily Ginsberg for help?"

"You can't win with that guy," he replied.

At that moment, Vasily Ginsberg's chauffeur brought him to University Hospital. It was lunchtime, and he made an unexpected visit to the office of Sasha Liebowitz. She was busy reviewing files when her assistant let him in. She was surprised to see him.

"I wanted to compliment you on the way you conducted yourself at the administrative hearing," he told her. "You did a beautiful job.

"I have never heard such a heartfelt, yet such a rational analysis before. You were very impressive."

"Thank you, Vasily, but I didn't mean to be. We've all been through hell. I was trying to express my outrage in a cogent, precise manner. I'm glad you approved."

"Why don't you join me for lunch," he said.

"I'm really very busy," she responded weakly. "I've got all this paperwork, and I have a staff meeting later in the day."

"I insist," said Ginsberg. "My chauffeur will drive us to Tio Pepe, the best Spanish restaurant in the city. Their fish and beef are excellent."

"Fine," she said with an awe-struck smile.

At the restaurant, Sanchez, the maitre d', greeted the couple.

"Hello, Mr. Ginsberg," he said, "and who is the lovely senorita?"

"This is Dr. Sasha Liebowitz," Ginsberg told him.

"How are you, Dr. Sasha?" inquired Sanchez.

"Fine."

"Mr. Ginsberg," said Sanchez, "do you want your regular table?"

"Yes."

At that point, Sanchez took him to a corner table by a large window that overlooked a courtyard that was planted with a beautiful arrangement of flowers.

"Do you want Severiano to wait on you today?" asked Sanchez.

"Yes," said Ginsberg.

A minute later, Severiano came over with the menus.

"You are looking well today, Mr. Ginsberg, and who is the beautiful senorita?"

"Severiano, this is Dr. Liebowitz."

"Buenos dias, senorita. But Mr. Ginsberg, the senorita is so gorgeous, I thought she was a model, not a doctor."

"You flatter me, Severiano," laughed Sasha.

"Beauty and brains," Severiano told Ginsberg, "such a rare combination!"

"Please keep up the flattery," said Sasha laughingly. "I think I can get used to this."

"What would you like for lunch today, Mr. Ginsberg and Dr. Liebowitz?"

"Do you like fish?" Ginsberg asked her.

"Yes."

"Severiano," Ginsberg asked, "how is the grouper?"

"Excellent."

"Sasha, try the grouper," Ginsberg told her.

"Okay."

"How about you, Mr. Ginsberg?"

"I'll have the tournedos, medium rare."

"Very good, and how about something to drink?"

"Pick out a nice rosé, for us, Severiano," said Ginsberg. "Surprise us."

"Si, senor."

"Again, Sasha, I would like to compliment you for the way you handled yourself at the hearing. You were very good and very impressive."

"Thank you."

"You know, I'm working on a lot of large deals. I haven't been here long, but I'm already establishing myself as a real force, a real player."

"Oh," she responded.

"You see," he went on, "in the post-war era I think we are in for an unprecedented wave of prosperity.

"Things are happening quickly. There will be more technological innovation, more consolidations, mergers and a greater need for capital and creative financing. This environment is made for me."

"You know," she responded, "you don't have the best reputation."

"Darling," he said as he grasped her hand, "people are jealous and they spread rumors. Do you think people would say anything about me if I weren't so successful?"

At that moment he continued to hold her hand tenderly and he stared into her eyes. His gaze broke down her defenses, and she was smitten by him, mesmerized in his presence.

"We would make a great couple," he said.

Sasha found it hard to talk as she returned his stare.

At that moment his cell phone rang.

"Hello," he said.

"I'm sorry, I can't talk now. I'll call you later."

"Who was that?" Sasha inquired.

"The president of Ugograd Telecommunications. He wants to invest with me."

"You didn't talk to him because you are with me?"

"Yes, darling."

He then leaned over and kissed her lightly on the lips.

At that instant, Severiano brought the wine and filled both glasses.

"To us," he told her as he and Sasha raised their glasses, and he clicked her glass with his.

Each drank.

"You're so lovely," he told her.

After some more staring and hand holding, Severiano brought the luncheon dishes.

"Tournedos for Mr. Ginsberg and grouper for the pretty doctor," he said, as he lay the dishes on the table.

"Enjoy," he said as he exited the table.

"Taste the grouper," Ginsberg told Sasha. "It is prepared like no fish you have ever eaten."

"Hmmm," she said, as she took her first bite. "Excellent choice, Vasily, I'm glad you suggested it. And how is yours?"

"Excellent, darling."

The couple finished the meal at a leisurely pace.

"How about dessert, Sasha?"

"Really, I've had enough."

"Try the pine nut cake," he said.

"Really, I can't eat anymore."

"I'll take a piece and give you some."

"Force me," she said, smiling.

"Severiano," ordered Ginsberg, "a slice of pine nut cake and two forks."

"Si, senor."

He brought the cake and Ginsberg cut it. "The first bite is for you, darling."

"It's delicious," she said, as Ginsberg held a fork up to her mouth and she bit into the cake.

"Would you want to try another taste?"

"One more," she said.

"That's it," she said as she finished her second bite.

"Isn't it outrageously good?" Ginsberg asked her.

"Absolutely, Vasily. Listen I must get back to the hospital. I have a busy day."

"Severiano," said Ginsberg, "the check, please."

"How will you pay for this?" he asked as he presented him the bill.

"Put it on my tab."

"Si, senor."

"How was your tournedos, Mr. Ginsberg?"

"Excellent, Severiano."

"And how was the beautiful doctor's grouper?"

"Wonderful."

As they walked outside to the limousine, Ginsberg asked Sasha, "How was your lunch?"

"Wonderful."

"And how was your afternoon?"

"Perfect, Vasily."

"Can I see you again?"

"Maybe."

"Can I call you?"

"Yes."

He held her hand on the way back to the hospital, and she rested her head on his shoulder. As they pulled up to the hospital, he embraced her and kissed her passionately on the lips. After several seconds, she pushed him away.

"I really have to get back," she said.

"Okay, Sasha, I will call you."

"Fine," she said.

When she came back to her office, Sasha's assistant said, "I didn't see you in the hospital restaurant for lunch. Where were you?"

"I was in heaven," she responded.

# Chapter XIII

# Difficult Times

Soon after Isadore Samonovich rented Sandler's Department Store, he began to notice pickets that carried placards which read: "Support Fair-trade Legislation." At first he paid little attention to the protesters, but in recent weeks the number of picketers had increased, and he began to worry.

Fair-trade legislation, he knew, would be aimed at his discounting policy and, if passed, would severely limit the way he did business. He understood that the Retail Merchants Association and the National Association of Manufacturers were behind the protest movement, and he heard that these organizations might be planning to have legislation introduced in the upcoming legislative session. Such legislation would enforce markups on goods at the wholesale and retail level and eliminate Samonovich's ability, as he called it, to utilize his "promotional pricing." He was alarmed.

One of his suppliers told him that the trade organizations would have a senator introduce a bill that would maintain markups. He asked his attorney, Yakov Potemkin, to look into the matter. Potemkin reported that indeed legislation was being readied for introduction. "What are we going to do?" he asked Potemkin.

"Fight it," he said. "We will have to get a copy of the bill when it is introduced, and then dissect it. We will have to attack it where we can. First, though, we will have to see what we're up against. Wait until the legislation is introduced," he advised.

Two weeks later the legislation, called the Retailers and Manufacturers Protection Bill, was introduced. It said: "The State, in the public interest, will establish a mechanism to enforce appropriate markups of merchandise as if all goods were manufactured in our country. If the manufacturer first, and the retailer second, does not recommend a markup, then the State will intervene and fix an appropriate markup. Appropriate pricing, or markups, will be maintained throughout the manufacturing and retail cycle."

Potemkin and Samonovich reviewed the bill together. "This is poor legislation," Potemkin told him. "It will be costly and difficult to enforce and will, in reality, establish a price-fixing mechanism, which may ultimately lead to a black market. Moreover, it will cause manufacturers, retailers and consumers to have less choice and will ultimately lead to higher prices. It will also stifle the merchants' and manufacturers' creativity."

Potemkin told him the legislation is being referred to the Economic Matters Committee of the House and Senate, where hearings will be held.

"Yakov," Samonovich said to him, "I want you to lobby against the legislation and be present at the hearings to testify against it."

"I will," he told his client.

As Potemkin began preparing to testify at the hearings, Samonovich, when one day crossing in front of a picketer, heard a voice. "Mr. Samonovich," the person said, "how are you?"

Samonovich recognized the person as Anastasiya Bunin. A month before she had come to his office to complain about some merchandise she had purchased. Samonovich intervened in a dispute she had with a department head. He replaced the original dress she had bought, much to her satisfaction. Samonovich then talked to her about her tastes and remembered she liked Paris imports.

"What are you doing here?" he asked her.

"I don't know," she replied. "My friend asked me to come down and walk around the store for an hour with this sign. Then she said we would have lunch and do some shopping."

"Where are you going to shop?" he asked.

"In your store, of course," she said.

"Why my store?"

"You have the best prices and merchandise."

"You know, Anastasiya, my father had an expression."

"What was that?"

"God watches over fools and drunks."

"What did he mean by that?"

"When you get a little older, you may find out."

As Samonovich turned to walk away, Anastasiyaa said to him, "Mr. Samonovich, I love to shop at Sandler's. It is my favorite thing to do."

"I appreciate that," he said as he made his way to his building. He turned to her and said, "Oh, by the way, those dresses, the Paris imports that you like so much, should be in next week."

"Thanks for letting me know, Mr. Samonovich. I'll be there."

"And thank you for shopping at Sandler's, Anastasiya."

Meanwhile, Potemkin prepared for the hearings. He began to contact other promotional stores which would be affected by the legislation. On one occasion, the lawyer for the Discount Mart called him and said this ruckus would never have started had not Samonovich leased Sandler's.

"Maybe the legislation should be called the 'Jew Bill,' instead of the Retailers and Manufacturers Protection Bill," said Potemkin sarcastically to the Discount Mart attorney. "This is some great country," Potemkin added. "A man rents an empty department store, and the state tries to put him out of business."

Potemkin also contacted SCALD (Senior Citizens Against Legislative Destruction). Potemkin told the group's executive vice-president, I. M. Andropov, that the organization should oppose the bill because it would force senior citizens, many of whom are on fixed incomes, to pay higher prices. He also enlisted the opposition of CC (Concerned Consumers).

Potemkin, representing Sandler's, would speak in opposition to the legislation at hearings that were scheduled to be conducted by the House and Senate Economic Matters Committee.

When the day of the Senate hearing convened, Potemkin read from carefully prepared notes. After speaking for twenty minutes, he concluded with this summation:

"We say we are a country which has traditionally had a free economy. Yet we seek to punish creativity and innovation. We will deprive merchants and manufacturers of pricing flexibility and creativity.

"We will add to the already high cost of government by creating a bureaucratic mechanism to administer laws that will be difficult to enforce because of the inevitable rise of the black markets.

"We will shackle the economy with unreasonable constraints.

"We will move away from free trade and lost-cost imports.

"We will make criminals of those who seek to circumvent unreasonable and, what will probably be, unenforceable laws.

"Lastly, we will deny consumers, retailers and manufacturers their logical choices; we will eliminate options for these groups; we will force higher prices on the economy; and we will constrain market forces from their natural and optimal directions.

"In short, I tell you this is harmful legislation which should be defeated by your committee. In reality, this legislation will benefit no one, because we are all eventually consumers, no matter what our religious beliefs are.

"Thank you."

Later that day the committee heard from other promotional retailers and senior-citizen lobbyists as well as distressed consumer groups.

Two days later, the Senate Economic Matters Committee voted to kill the bill. Effectively, the legislation had died in committee.

Several days later, Potemkin, while in his office, got a call from Vasily Ginsberg, who phoned him from his limousine.

"Nice work, old man," he said. "You did a good job before the committee. You were very skillful and logical. You also did a solid lobbying job. You deserve to be commended, old man."

"Thank you," replied Potemkin.

"Old man, one day I will try you out and send some legal business your way."

"Fine," Potemkin replied.

Ginsberg then hung up.

"What a piece of dreck," Potemkin said to himself as the phone call ended. He then muttered to himself, "Thirty Jews in town and I already need associates."

It was a little after 5 p.m., and Ginsberg told his chauffeur to drive to University Hospital. He decided to take a chance and see if Sasha Liebowitz was in her office. When he arrived, he found the support staff was gone. He walked to her office and knocked on the door.

"Come in," he heard her say. As he entered, Sasha said, "Vasily, what are you doing here?"

"I'm here to see you, darling. It's been over a month since we were last together. Why haven't you returned my calls?"

"I've been busy."

"Nobody's that busy, darling."

"Look, it's getting late. I must be getting home. Levi is expecting me. Call me tomorrow."

"Okay," he said as he left the office.

Several days later, he called her from his office.

"How about having dinner with me tonight?" he asked her.

"I can't."

"How about tomorrow?"

105

"Yes. Pick me up at the office at 6 p.m."

He arrived on time. "You look exquisite, darling. How do you maintain your freshness and loveliness after working all day?"

Sasha just looked into his eyes, absorbed by his presence.

"Please come," he said. "My chauffeur is waiting." He took her arm and escorted her to his limousine.

"We have reservations at Dimitri's," he said.

"I'm not familiar with that place, Vasily."

"It's excellent. They know me there. They always roll out the red carpet for me.

"How have things been at the hospital?"

"Hectic."

"How so?"

"Heavy case loads. Difficult surgeries. Continual monitoring. It's a tense profession. Life and death resides with me. The pressure can be awful."

"How do you unwind?"

"Who can unwind? You go to sleep with it. You wake up with it. You think it. You are a twenty-four hour a day office. Plus I do my best to keep a house and keep Levi happy."

"Can I be of help?"

"That was thoughtful of you."

"We will be at Dimitri's soon. Relax, unwind, and enjoy yourself. Everyone needs peace and quiet."

"I'll say," she said.

When they arrived, Alexander, the maitre d', greeted Ginsberg: "Mr. Ginsberg, so good to see you. Your table is waiting."

"Who will be serving tonight?" he asked Alexander.

"Gus."

"Excellent."

Alexander escorted the couple to their table, which was next to a replica of a waterfall. Gus soon brought the menus.

"What do you recommend?" Sasha asked Gus.

Before he could answer, Ginsberg said, "Sasha, let's split the Greek salad."

"That's fine."

"Do you like snapper?" he then asked her.

"What are you suggesting?"

"Try the skaras. That's their snapper."

"Okay."

"Gus," he said. "Skaras for two."

"Anything to drink?" Gus asked.

"Bring us your best white wine," Ginsberg said. "You know my taste."

"Fine," he said.

As Gus left the table, Ginsberg said, "It seems to me you are going to have to find a better way to balance relaxation and pleasure with work."

"It's easier said than done."

"Maybe I could help."

"How?"

"If you got to know me better, you could find out.

"You see," he continued, "I travel in a larger world. I could do things for you. With me, you would see a side of life you have only imagined."

"How is that going to help the fact that we have a shortage of doctors in this country? I have a responsibility."

"Like I say, I can do things for you that you never anticipated."

"You still haven't answered the question."

With that the salad arrived. Gus poured the wine which he had brought previously but had stayed unopened.

"This is delicious," Sasha said as she took a sip.

"Try the salad," Ginsberg said.

"Hmmm," she said as she took her first bite. "I love this feta cheese. Everything is so good: the tomatoes, scallions and especially the olives and anchovies. I didn't know a Greek salad could taste like this."

"You don't know a lot of things. Like I say, I can open a whole world for you. In business, I'm a star. I'm treated like a star. I travel like a star. I do things like a star. When I do deals, the world watches. Then it applauds.

"There is nothing humdrum about my existence."

As she finished her salad, Ginsberg grasped her hand.

"Come along with me," he told her.

She began to blush, at first speechless and then embarrassed in his presence. She was at a loss as to how to respond. She was unable to find words to express herself. She felt uneasy and awkward.

When the main course came, she felt relieved.

"I hope the skaras is as good as the Greek salad," Sasha said, finally able to speak.

"Everything I touch is the best, Sasha, including you. You're beautiful; you're intelligent. Come with me. Life is meant to be lived. The difference between me and you is that I dictate. I'm not dictated to. I lead. I don't follow.

"Come with me," he said as he regrasped her hand.

"I'm feeling so awkward. You know I'm with someone."

"Leave him," he replied. "Come with me."

"Uh, the food looks delicious, Vasily."

He stared at her coldly, annoyed at her reaction.

Thankful that the food had arrived so the tenor of conversation might change, Sasha began to cut into her skaras.

"This is wonderful, Vasily," she said as she took her first bite. "How is yours?"

"Fine," he said sharply and abruptly with a distinct irritation in his voice.

"This is so good," she repeated. "How do they prepare this?"

Unprepared for the change in the emotion of their conversation, he began to brood inwardly.

When Gus came over to ask how the meal was, Sasha queried him as to how the skaras was prepared.

"The secret," Gus said, "is that we brush the fish with oil and we grill it until it is lightly charred. We are able to cook it through but still serve it moist. We add lemon and parsley. When we do all that, we are able to serve a fish with a crisp skin and a sweet flavor, while keeping it, as I said, moist."

"How interesting," said Sasha.

"Don't you find that interesting, Vasily?" she said.

He nodded solemnly.

"I will be back to see how you are doing," Gus said.

"Thank you, Gus," Sasha replied.

Ginsberg again nodded solemnly.

The two finished their meal in silence.

At the end of the meal, Gus asked about dessert.

"Sasha, if you want dessert, try the cheesecake," said Ginsberg.

"Good choice," said Gus.

"Is it all right if we split a piece, Vasily?" asked Sasha.

"Sure," said Ginsberg, as his spirits brightened. "And Gus, bring two coffees."

"Certainly."

As the two ate the piece of cheesecake, Ginsberg asked Sasha if she would like to accompany him to the Club Infinity, where they could listen to music and dance.

"Sure," she said.

The answer surprised him and his mood continued to brighten.

As the two took small bites from the cake, Ginsberg signaled to Gus for the check.

He got it, charged the bill on his credit card and left a generous tip, also on his credit card.

"Come, Sasha, let's go. You'll enjoy the club," he said.

She finished her coffee and he held her hand as he escorted her to his limousine.

A few minutes later, they were at the Club Infinity. They had a table near the dance floor. He ordered a vodka and tonic, she a glass of wine.

A slow song was playing. He asked her to dance. He held her tightly as they moved to the rhythms of the music. He was surprised at her sense of rhythm and how she flowed to the beat of the music. By the time the music ended, her head lay on his shoulder. "I enjoyed that," she said. "I haven't danced in the longest time."

They stayed on the dance floor waiting for the next song. This time a faster song played. Again Sasha moved exquisitely to the rhythms of the music. Her movements flowed in a sequence that first anticipated and then matched the beat of the song. Her movements seemed almost professional. He felt awkward and upstaged in her presence. Other patrons began to stare at her. When Ginsberg realized this, he began to feel embarrassed. Thankful that the music had ended, he almost pleaded with her to sit the next number out.

"I haven't done this in the longest time. I'm just beginning to enjoy myself," she said.

"You're wearing me out," he replied. "Where did you learn to dance like that?"

"Like what?"

"Like what you do, Sasha."

"I didn't know I was doing anything special."

As the two sat down, he said, "You know, the more I'm with you, the more I want to stay with you."

"How are your business deals coming?" she said as she tried to redirect the topic of conversation. "You've been awfully quiet about them tonight."

"Fantastic," he said. "They are the next best thing to having a license to print money.

"I'm going to need someone to join me for the ride."

"Oh," she responded.

"Yes," he said, "big things are meant to be shared."

At that point, a slow song began to play and a patron from an adjoining table asked Sasha to dance.

"I'd be delighted," she said.

Ginsberg got up politely as Sasha stood up and the couple made their way to the dance floor. As she returned to the table, Ginsberg kept telling her about his big plans. She seemed uninterested, almost bored.

"Can't we talk about something else?" she said.

"Like what?" he said. "In my life there is little else but business and you."

"It's getting late," she said. "I have a busy day tomorrow. I really should be getting home."

"I wish you were going home with me."

"That's sweet of you."

As the limousine made its way to Sasha's residence, Ginsberg asked her if he could call her this week.

"Yes," she said.

"Did you enjoy yourself tonight?" he asked.

"Yes," she responded again.

"You didn't show it."

"I felt it," she said.

"You did?"

"Yes."

He then grabbed her and kissed her passionately. In turn, the passion of her embrace equaled his, as did the feeling and emotion of her kiss.

"I'll call you this week," he told her.

"That's fine."

"Good night," he said.

"Good night, darling," she told him as she grabbed him and kissed him passionately, taking him by complete surprise.

She left the limousine and walked to her apartment.

As she walked in, Bushkin sat in the living room waiting for her.

"Where have you been?" he asked.

"Out," she said.

"With whom?"
"Vasily Ginsberg."
"That again."
"Yes, that again," she said.

# Chapter XIV

# Life After Levi

"Sasha, what's wrong? I've never seen you look like that," said her assistant, Nadia Pavel.

"I haven't slept, and I'm going to need an apartment to stay in. It's over between Levi and me."

"What?"

"It ended this morning."

"I thought you two were the ideal couple. Weren't you going to be married?"

"Well, he never really asked, but everyone assumed so, including me."

"Can I talk to you, Nadia?"

"Yes."

"I have a light morning," Sasha said, "let's go to the hospital restaurant to talk. I'm a wreck."

"Please get a table, Sasha. I'll be along in a few minutes, right after I return these phone calls."

"I will meet you down there," Sasha replied. "Please don't be too long. I'm very upset."

Minutes later Nadia joined Sasha in a private corner booth, far from the other patrons. The two ordered coffee which a waitress immediately brought over.

After Nadia took her first sip, she asked Sasha, "What happened?"

"Vasily Ginsberg, the financier, kept pursuing me. He's very good looking and very rich. He wouldn't take no for an answer," said Sasha.

"About a month ago he took me to lunch at Tio Pepe. He came with his limousine. He flattered me and said all the right things. I didn't want to take it beyond that.

"Then, however, he began calling me. I didn't return the phone calls. He showed up one night when I was working late and asked me to dinner. I refused. Eventually, though, we made a date, which was last night. We had dinner at Dimitri's and then went dancing. I got home late and Levi was waiting for me. I told him where I had been and with whom.

"Then it started."

"What?" said Nadia.

"He screamed and carried on like a raving maniac."

"And what did you do?" said Nadia.

"I screamed back. We both said things I know we now regret. But in the heat of the moment things are said--and they are the wrong things."

"What did he tell you?" interrupted Nadia.

"That I can't be trusted. That I'm immature and disloyal. And that this is very hurtful to him."

"Did he say he loved you?"

"Yes. Then he said that his love was 'misplaced' and that he 'made a bad choice.'"

"Then what did he do?"

"He told me to get out and that it was over."

"Is that all he said?"

"Well, before he said that, he told me how he thought he was so lucky to have found me. I was his ideal: intelligent, beautiful, everything he could ask for.

"Nadia, Levi thinks there is more going on than there actually is--that this is some full-blown affair."

"I feel very bad for the both of you," said Nadia. "Is there anything I can do?"

"Just listen, please."

"Do you know the circumstances in which Levi and I met?"

"No," said Nadia.

"After the Holocaust, he found me hiding in a mountain outside of Tashni. We were both extraordinarily lucky to be alive. It was as if fate threw us together. Our families had been murdered, and we needed each other desperately.

"We took to each other. We were compatible. We enjoyed each other's company.

"We fell in love without having a traditional romance. Things happened so quickly. One day I was literally hiding in a mountain, trying to stay alive. The next day I was living with him. When the Jewish survivors started coming to Ugograd, one was Vasily Ginsberg. He started coming on to me immediately, and I enjoyed his attention.

"He began to ask me out and sent flowers and called. At that point Levi gave me an ultimatum: 'It's Vasily Ginsberg or me,' he said. So I told Vasily I was with someone, and his intentions toward me had to end."

"Isn't Levi under a lot of pressure?" asked Nadia.

"Well, yes. In addition to his teaching position at University, he is the acting rabbi to our small congregation. He is such a decent, loving guy. He's so dutiful, so sincere, so honest about everything."

"What does he think of Vasily?"

"He can't stand him. He literally recoils from him in his midst. He doesn't trust him and has told me so."

"What do you think of Vasily?"

"I am very attracted to him. It's almost like an infatuation, a crush. The circles he travels in, the way he carries himself, it's all so new and exciting."

"What do you think of Levi?"

"I really love him. In many ways we're a perfect match: similar upbringings and families. It was like we're meant to be. It may sound crazy, but I'd rather live with Levi and be out with Vasily.

"I don't know what's worse, having no choice or too many choices. I wish my father were alive to talk to."

"Would you listen to him?"

"I don't know."

"Sasha, let me tell you one thing about forbidden fruit."

"What's that?"

"The first bite tastes great. After that, it's all downhill."

Sasha paused, so as to extract all possible meaning from Nadia's last words.

Then Sasha said, "Thanks for listening to me. It's getting late. I have to get back to the office and so do you."

"Sasha, if you need a place to stay tonight, my home is available."

"Thanks."

She returned to her office and went through her phone messages.

One was from Vasily Ginsberg and her mood brightened a bit.

"Vasily, it's Sasha," she said as she called him on his private line.

"Darling, I was worried about you. The receptionist said you were with Nadia and that you weren't looking too well."

"I'm okay, now."

"Is there anything wrong?"

"Well, no. I mean yes."

"What is it?"

"It's over between Levi and me. I feel terrible."

"Is there anything I can do?"

"Just let me be. Please, just let me be."

Several days later, Ginsberg called her again.

"How do you feel today?" he asked.

"Better, I'm getting over it, I think," she said.

"Is there anything I can do?" he asked again.

"No," she answered.

"How about joining me for dinner tonight?"

"Can we make it tomorrow night? I'm just getting situated in a new apartment."

"Certainly, darling. I will pick you up at the hospital, say 5 p.m."

"Fine," she said.

At 5 p.m., Ginsberg knocked on her office door.

As he walked in he said, "Darling, how's the world's most beautiful doctor?" The words were a temporary elixir. She relaxed and smiled beautifully in his presence.

He kissed her lightly on his cheek and said, "You look especially attractive tonight. Tell me, darling, is there a time you don't look like heavenly perfection, although the heavens pale in comparison to your beauty."

Her smile widened with his words.

"I have a special treat for us tonight, darling. We will dine at my townhouse. My staff will attend to our needs."

As they drove toward his house in his chauffeur-driven limousine, he asked Sasha, "What would you like for dinner? I'll phone ahead."

"I don't know," she said. "Whatever you like."

"How about chicken Kiev?"

"Fine."

"Hello, Mikhail, I will be dining with Dr. Liebowitz tonight. Please prepare chicken Kiev for two with a caesar salad. And pick out a dry champagne from the wine cellar. Dr. Liebowitz is very, very special to me."

"Vasily, you always know what to say. I hope I can be good company tonight. I have been through a lot in a short time. I'm very depressed."

"Darling, I'm here for you. Your problems are my problems. I want to help you."

"Oh, Vasily, why is everything so complicated?"

"Let me be your bridge to a new life. Come into my world."

As his chauffeur drove up to his townhouse, Vasily and Sasha exited the limousine. He held her hand. They proceeded to the front door. Ginsberg's servant opened the door as they approached.

"Good evening, sir."

"Good evening, ma'am," his servant said.

"Good evening, Artim," Ginsberg said. "This is Dr. Liebowitz."

"Pleased to meet you, ma'am."

"A pleasure to meet you, Artim."

The two took the elevator to the second-floor dining area. Mikhail met them as the elevator door opened.

"Good evening, sir," he said. "Dinner will be ready in twenty minutes."

"Call us when it is ready," said Ginsberg. "We will be sitting by the fireplace."

"Dr. Liebowitz," Mikhail said, "may I take your coat?"

"Certainly," she said. He then took the coat off her shoulders and folded it over his arm with a technical proficiency that indicated his long experience with such gentlemanly maneuvers.

The two sat on the sofa by the fireplace, where the fire provided a soothing warmth. Ginsberg took Sasha's hand. "Don't worry, darling," he told her. "Everything will be fine."

"I hope so, Vasily. I feel a deep sense of loss."

"You'll get over it," he replied. "I'll help you. I'm so fond of you. You are my one and only." He then kissed her lightly on the lips. She stared into his eyes, and she kissed him lightly on his cheek. He then held his arm tightly around her shoulders.

The two stared into the fire and exchanged several more kisses.

"Dinner is served," said Mikhail.

"It's times like this," said Ginsberg, "that I wish I was never hungry."

"Me, too," she said.

As the two approached the dining-room table, Sasha said, "Vasily, your home is beautiful."

"My decorator, Anton, can translate my instructions into beautiful reality. His talents are exquisite."

"Mikhail," said Ginsberg next, "please hold Dr. Liebowitz's chair."

"Certainly, sir."

With the two seated, Mikhail brought the champagne and caesar salad. He poured the champagne and served the salad.

"Taste your salad, Sasha," said Ginsberg.

"It's unbelievable," she said.

"Mikhail has a special recipe," laughed Ginsberg. "But he won't share it with me. Try your champagne, Sasha."

"Delightful," she replied after she took a small sip.

"How do you feel now?"

"Better."

"With me," he answered, "feeling better will be a way of life. It will be a thing of permanence and beauty."

The two finished their dinners in silence.

"How was your meal, darling?" Ginsberg asked.

"Perfect," she said.

Ginsberg then rang for Mikhail.

"What have you planned for dessert?" he asked him.

"Chocolate mousse, sir."

"Mikhail," said Ginsberg, "bring it over to the fire. We will be sitting on the sofa with our drinks."

"Yes, sir."

"I will join you by the fire, Vasily, but really I can't eat any more," she said.

"Try some of the dessert. Chocolate mousse is Mikhail's specialty."

"To tell you the truth," Sasha said, "I don't think I ever had it before."

"You'll love it," he said.

When the mousse arrived, Vasily fed it to her.

"This is delicious."

"Try one more, dear," he said as he fed her some more.

"Wonderful, Vasily, but I can't eat any more."

"Sir," Mikhail interrupted.

"What is it?" said Ginsberg agitatedly.

"Sir, Malcolm Bolt is on the phone from London. He says it's an emergency."

"Tell him to call me in the office tomorrow," Ginsberg said.

"The night is young, Sasha, what do you want to do now? Would you want to stay and listen to a Rachmaninoff piano concerto or take a ride? I could have my chauffeur meet us in front with the limousine."

"How about a nice walk?" she said.

"Okay. I could use the exercise," he said.

"Mikhail, bring Dr. Liebowitz her coat."

"Yes, sir."

"May I help you on with your coat, Dr. Liebowitz?" said Mikhail.

As Mikhail helped her on with her coat, she smiled awkwardly, embarrassed by the attention.

When the two exited the townhouse, Vasily said, "Sasha, I know you're going through a lot, but I'm falling in love with you. What can I do to fulfill you, to make your life as beautiful as you are."

"Just be yourself," she said.

"What do you mean by that?"

"Just what I said," replied Sasha.

"What do you like to do?" he asked her.

"Almost anything. I enjoy the theatre, music, art, and athletic events."

"Do you like to sail?

"I've only been a couple of times," she said.

"When my yacht is ready, I plan to do some cruising on the Mediterranean. You'll love the water. It is relaxing and the sea is beautiful."

"That's nice," she said.

"Are you all right?" he asked her.

"I'm fine, just a little depressed."

"I can understand that. Would you want to be my guest and stay the night in my townhouse?"

"It's too soon, Vasily."

"I see," he said.

"Really, it's getting late. Can your chauffeur drive me home?"

"Certainly. I will go with you."

As the two sat in the back of the limousine, each said little. Sasha began to feel an awkwardness that she couldn't express. As she tried to rationalize things, Sasha realized that she never really had a conversation with Vasily.

With him, everything seemed so staged, so contrived. When she thought about that, she became tense and her body stiffened and became rigid.

"Am I a prop to him?" she asked herself. "Am I a trophy? Am I a human version of a piece of art on the wall? Why can't I talk to him?"

The limousine pulled up in front of her apartment building. Ginsberg reached over to kiss her on her lips. She turned her face and he ended up kissing her cheek.

"Isn't this near where you and Levi lived?" Ginsberg asked.

"Yes. It's also near the hospital," she said.

"Can I show you to your apartment?"

"I'll be all right. I am sorry if I wasn't good company tonight," she said. "I'm very sorry."

As she entered her building alone, she got on the elevator and thought about what her assistant, Nadia Pavel, told her. When she walked into her apartment, those words echoed in her ear: "Sasha, let me tell you about forbidden fruit: The first bite tastes great. After that, it's all downhill."

Then Sasha began to cry.

# Chapter XV

## Passover

Sasha knew with Passover approaching she would likely find Bushkin in his study early in the evening. When she approached the synagogue, she saw his office light on. She knocked on the door.

"Come in," he said.

She walked in. He was startled to see her, as it had been a month since she had moved out.

He looked at her icily and said, "Can I help you?"

"May I borrow two Haggadahs for the Passover holidays?" she asked. Without saying a word he left the office and brought back two books which he handed her. He returned to his desk and continued his paper work without acknowledging her presence.

She said, "I plan to have a Seder with Vasily Ginsberg."

Still not looking up, he said, "I didn't know caviar had been added to the Passover plate."

"Things aren't what they seem," she replied, speaking rapidly as she said those words.

"Oh," he paused, "What are they? I hear you two are Mr. and Ms. Couple, real stars of the social scene."

"If you don't care about me, why do you ask?" she said, once again accelerating the pace of her speech.

"I don't ask," he replied. "People tell me you two are Mr. and Ms. Glamorous."

"Why are you being such a smart ass?" she said.

"I'm being the smart ass," he said angrily. "Who was it that began running around?"

"Levi, it wasn't what it seemed."

"The hell it wasn't, you goddamn liar."

"Look, Levi, can't we be friends?"

"No. Please leave. I'm busy. If you don't hurry, you may miss Mr. Ginsberg's chauffeur and then, who knows, his yacht."

"That wasn't necessary," she said.

"If you hadn't started running around, we would have been married. You know I really loved you, but you were disloyal. I still have the engagement ring I was going to give you."

She looked down at the floor, unable to fashion a response. Finally, after several seconds of trying, she got up and left without saying a word. She was distraught. He was angry.

Three days before the scheduled Seder at the synagogue, the congregation's board of directors convened to review its finances and go over plans for the Seder.

Except for Vasily Ginsberg and Sasha, all were present: Isadore and Yetta Samonovich, Tatyana Samuelson, Yakov and Sarah Potemkin, Amos Sephard and Bushkin. After the meeting started, Vasily Ginsberg walked in. As he did, and was about to sit down, Levi Bushkin spotted him.

"Get the hell out of here you phony son-of-a-bitch," he yelled at him. "Get out," he repeated as his face reddened with rage.

Yakov Potemkin put his arms around Bushkin so as to restrain him.

Isadore Samonovich then walked over to Ginsberg to apologize and said it might be best if he left. Ginsberg did, while Potemkin still had his arms around Bushkin.

Then Bushkin walked outside to compose himself. Able to do so, he returned five minutes later to reconvene the meeting.

"Get a grip on yourself," Yakov Potemkin told him. "We can't have our rabbi verbally abusing and then assaulting members of our congregation. We have enough problems."

Without acknowledging Potemkin's admonition, Bushkin began to work through the agenda.

"With fifty members now," he told the directors, "we may be able to go to an annual dues' structure, with, of course, larger contributions welcomed. What I suggest is that a committee, composed of me, Isadore Samonovich, and Yakov Potemkin, be formed to recommend a dues' structure that the board of directors can vote on at the next meeting. All in favor, say aye." After a voice vote he said, "the motion carries."

Next Bushkin said, "We will have our first communal Seder. Hopefully, this will be an annual event."

"Yetta," asked Bushkin, "have you finished all the Seder plates?"

"Yes," she said.

"Amos, you know to have the extra Matzoh here."

"Yes."

"Tatyana, you know to bring the wine."

"Yes."

"Sarah, you will be responsible for the chicken dinners."

"Yes."

"Yakov, your son, Joshua, knows he will say the Four Questions."

"He better," Yakov replied.

"Okay," said Bushkin, "we're ready. I will act as a leader and, following the Seder, I will have a few brief words to say."

"Please keep your comments brief," said Yakov. "At the end, we will all be tired and likely full of wine."

"Point well taken," said Bushkin.

The night of the Seder, Bushkin greeted all the congregants amiably. Sasha Liebowitz and Vasily Ginsberg were conspicuous by their absence. Bushkin began the Seder commemorating the exodus from Egyptian bondage.

He turned to Yakov Potemkin for an explanation of the items on the Passover plate: the three Matzos, Roasted Shankbone, Roasted Egg, Moror, Charoses and Karpas. Potemkin gave particular emphasis to the Matzos, Moror and Charoses, all symbols of Egyptian bondage.

Potemkin said: "Four times, in the course of the Service, we shall partake of the wine, symbol of joy and thanksgiving. The four cups represent the four-fold promise which the Lord made to the Israelites in Egypt. In the following words, He assured them they would be freed from servitude: 'I will bring you forth; I will deliver you; I will redeem you; I will take you.'"

Bushkin then read from the Haggadah: "These are the symbols of Passover--echoes of the past and reminders for the present. As we partake of them, may we remember the events which they recall, and may we embody their spirit in our present-day endeavors. We shall now sanctify the holiday with the recitation of Kiddush. Let us rise."

After the Kiddush, the assembled had their first glass of wine.

As the service proceeded, Joshua Potemkin, eight years old, approached Bushkin. Now standing next to him, Joshua said, "Mah neesh-ta-noh ha-lai-loh hazeh mee-kol hay-lay-los?"

"Why is the night of Passover different from all other nights of the year?"

As Joshua said the Four Questions, Yakov mouthed each word in silence. Sarah Potemkin became teary eyed. At the end of the passage, Yakov smiled widely.

"I didn't know Yakov could smile," Amos Shepard whispered to Isadore Samonovich.

"Only when he is not working," replied Samonovich.

"He must smile when he sends those bills," said Sephard.

Bushkin turned to Joshua and said, "We shall now answer the four basic questions concerning Passover, which you have asked."

Assembled: Once we were slaves to Pharaoh in Egypt, and the Lord, in His goodness and mercy, brought us forth from that land, with a mighty hand and an outstretched arm.

Bushkin: Had He not rescued us from the hand of the despot, surely we and our children would still be enslaved, deprived of liberty and human dignity.

Assembled: We, therefore, gather year after year, to retell this ancient story. For, in reality, it is not

129

ancient, but eternal in its message, and its spirit. It proclaims man's burning desire to preserve liberty and justice for all.

Bushkin: The first question asked concerns the use of Matzoh. We eat these unleavened cakes to remember that our ancestors, in their haste to leave Egypt, could not wait for breads to rise, and so removed them from the ovens while still flat.

Assembled: We partake of the Moror on this night that we might taste of some bitterness, to remind ourselves how bitter is the lot of one caught in the grip of slavery.

Bushkin: We dip twice in the course of this Service, greens in salt water and Moror in Charoses, once to replace tears with gratefulness, and once to sweeten bitterness and suffering.

Assembled: The fourth question asks why, on this night, we eat in a reclining position. To recline at mealtimes in ancient days was the sign of a free man. On this night of Passover, we demonstrate our sense of complete freedom by reclining during our repast.

Bushkin then proceeded with the service: The Four Sons, The Lord's Promise, The Story of Israel in the Land of Egypt, The Ten Plagues, Dayaynoo, The Three Symbols of Passover, and the passage of Our Personal Deliverance.

After another Kiddush, the assembled drank the wine. Bushkin then distributed pieces of broken Matzoh to everyone present. He said the Ha-motsi.

Bushkin next distributed the Moror combined with the Charoses. He said, "We shall now partake of the Moror, combined with the Charoses. Thus, we remember how bitter is slavery, and how it can be sweetened by God's redemption."

He recited another Bracha.

He then had pieces of broken Matzoh passed out to the congregants. He told each to place the bitter herbs between two pieces of Matzoh and said, in unison with members of the congregation, "In ancient times, the revered sage, Hillel, observed, literally, the Biblical Commandment concerning the eating of the Pesach with Matzoh and Moror. It is stated: 'With Matzoh and Moror shall they eat it.' Thus, did he combine them, even as we now do, and ate them together."

"We will now eat the Passover dinner."

"None too soon," Amos Sephard said to Yakov Potemkin.

"In turn," Potemkin said to Sephard, "How did you like the way Joshua said the Four Questions?"

"Very good," said Sephard. "Very good. Now pass the chicken, please."

After he did, Yakov began to make the rounds. "Levi, how did you like the way Joshua said the Four Questions?"

"Like a rabbi to be," he said.

"Isadore, what do you think of my eight-year-old son?"

"He's the boy wonder," he replied.

"And Yetta, how about you?"

"That young man will bring you much nachas. I can tell. I know."

"Tatyana, what do you think of my Josh?"

"He's got a voice like an angel."

"Yakov, sit down," said his wife, Sarah. "You're making a pest of yourself."

"Can't I enjoy myself?" he said.

"Mommy."

"What is it, Rachel?"

"Josh said when I get older I'm going to get pimples and I'm going to be ugly."

"You tell your older brother if he doesn't stop, he will be punished for a month."

"Josh," Rachel yelled across the room, "Mommy said you're in trouble."

Meanwhile, Joshua already finished his first helping and was the first in line for seconds.

"He's eating too much, Yakov," said Sarah. "Please talk to him. He's starting to get heavy.

"But don't be hard on him. You know how sensitive he is."

"He gets that from my side of the family," replied Yakov.

"Let's not get into that," said Sarah. "Your side couldn't spell 'sensitive.'"

Amos Sephard and Tatyana Samuelson approached Bushkin.

"I'm glad we had this Seder," Tatyana said to Bushkin.

"I echo that," said Sephard. "I think in time we will have a thriving Jewish community, which will be in no small measure a testament to your leadership and commitment."

"Thank you both," he said as he hugged each warmly.

"Uh-oh," said Sephard.

"What is it?" said Bushkin.

"Yakov is coming over," said Sephard. "I'll handle this."

"Yakov, for the fourth time, Josh was great."

Potemkin, acknowledging the words, walked by and widened his smile.

Sarah Potemkin now approached Bushkin.

"Levi," she told him, "you're a beautiful human being, and I hope everything works out for the best between you and Sasha. In my heart I know you love her and she loves you."

He smiled at her wistfully but was unable to speak. The two embraced. Sarah then felt a tug on her dress.

"What is it, Rachel?" she asked.

"Josh said I was a tattletale."

"You tell him if he doesn't behave, I'm really going to punish him."

"He said you always say that and you never really do anything."

"You tell him this time I really, really mean it."

"Josh," Rachel yelled across the room, "Mommy said this time you're really, really in trouble and this time she means it."

"Oh, no," Sarah said.

"What is it?" replied Bushkin.

"Josh is in line again. This is his third helping. He is going to get heavy. I know it. I just know it."

Sarah then continued, "Listen, Levi, it would be Yakov's and my greatest pleasure to come to your and Sasha's bris."

Unable to fashion a response, he re-embraced Sarah.

Now composed, he said, "I appreciate your words. They are very thoughtful. I know you mean well."

With dinner complete, the Afikomen (pieces of Matzoh) was passed out. Afikomen, Bushkin reminded the congregants, means dessert.

The third glass of wine was poured and drunk.

Bushkin then read the passage of Elijah the Prophet: "Jewish tradition states that Elijah's greatest mission shall come when the Messiah will appear on earth, to usher in the long-promised era of permanent peace and tranquility. For, it will be Elijah, the Prophet, who will precede the Messiah and will announce his arrival and, with it, the arrival of freedom and peace for all men."

Yakov Potemkin then said: "On this Seder night, when we pray for freedom, we invoke the memory of the beloved Elijah. May his spirit enter our home at this hour, and every home, bringing a message of hope for the future, faith in the goodness of men, and the assurance that freedom will come to all. We now welcome Elijah, beloved guest at our Seder, as we rise."

The door is opened for Elijah.

The assembled say in unison: "Direct Thy wrath, O God, upon evil and persecution. Protect Thy people, Israel, from those who destroy them. May the spirit of Elijah, who enters our home at this hour, enter the hearts of all men. May he inspire them to love Thee, and may he fill them with the desire to build a good world, one in which justice and freedom shall be the inheritance of all."

Following a fourth glass of wine, Bushkin concluded the service.

"I would like to thank you all for coming," he said. "Tonight, during our Seder, we commemorated the story of our Egyptian bondage, the exodus, and through Elijah, the Prophet, we seek to look optimistically towards a better future.

"Needless to say, this Passover service and Seder have eerie parallels to our own lives. With the onset of hostilities, we were either rounded up or forced into hiding to avoid death. Like our enslaved ancestors, we led lives of quiet desperation and uncertainty.

"When the war ended, we received amnesty. Our ancestors, upon their exodus from Egypt, found the promised land. Now we live in peace and enjoy, or pursue, prosperity.

"Furthermore, like the ancient Israelites, we chose not to abandon our faith. Instead, we live as Jews.

"May we always be able to do so, and may we meet here again on the next Passover."

"Amen!"

# Chapter XVI

## Sonia

"I've been invited to attend the first post-war meeting of the World Jewish Congress, in New York. I will act as a representative of our country," Bushkin told the congregation's board of directors. "To fund this trip, what I propose is that I pay half and the congregation pay half."

Yakov Potemkin polled the other directors present: his wife, Sarah, Amos Sephard, Tatyana Samuelson, and Isadore and Yetta Samonovich. All approved the request.

Potemkin added, "Please note in the minutes, Yetta, that the congregation's money is to be spent prudently, and we reserve the right to audit the expenses."

"Was that necessary?" responded Bushkin angrily, as he glared at Potemkin.

"Don't be so sanctimonious," Potemkin said to him.

"Sanctimonious. Who was it that took the lead and formed this congregation; acted as the rabbi; contributed dues; and never asked for a nickel in compensation?

"You have your nerve, Yakov."

"I'm sorry," he said.

"Apology accepted."

"Yetta, please don't put in the minutes what I was about to tell Yakov."

The directors laughed and the momentary tension was broken.

"When is the conference?" Amos Sephard asked him.

"In August."

"It's hot in New York at that time," Sephard replied.

"I know," Bushkin said.

At the University Hospital, Nadia Pavel, Sasha's assistant, asked her where she was going on vacation.

"I'm going on a Mediterranean cruise on Vasily Ginsberg's private yacht."

"How exclusive," said Nadia.

"Do you want to take my place?" said Sasha.

"What?"

"You heard me; do you want to take my place?"

"What's the problem?"

"I'm in a relationship that's going nowhere and isn't right for me. I was a fool."

"Why do you say that?"

"I'm an ornament," she replied. "A picture on the wall. A piece of sculpture. A notch on his belt. I'm what's fashionable for him today.

"Tomorrow I'll be out of fashion. He'll have a need to be seen with a Princess Petrushka or a Lady Liviniski or a Countess Corasova."

"But Sasha, you are always pictured with Vasily on the Informant's Society Page at charity balls, restaurants, and art shows. You look so happy and glamorous together."

"Since when do you believe what you read in the paper? Vasily Ginsberg knows how to court the press and orchestrate publicity. It's all part of a facade--part of a big myth. His motivation is to keep his name in front of the public. He does this well. Whether you believe it or not, I'm part of his image-enhancement process. I'm like a soldier in his publicity army. We happen to photograph well together, that's all.

"The man has no substance," continued Sasha. "We've never had an in-depth conversation. I don't think he's capable of one.

"He's a master manipulator, and I've been manipulated to further his ends."

"If you feel that way, why are you going on the cruise?" said Nadia.

"By being with him, I earned this vacation. Besides, the rest will do me good."

"Aren't you being hypocritical?"

"Certainly. But I've had a good teacher."

"That's pretty cynical," replied Nadia.

"Maybe so, but I'm going."

Bushkin's plane touched down at Newark Airport. He disembarked, got a cab and told the driver to take him to the Metropolitan Building at Fifth Avenue and Fifty-fifth Street.

Traffic was heavy. He immediately noticed the quality of the cab and inquired as to the make and model, because he felt Amos Sephard could have an interest in such a vehicle. However, the multi-lingual Bushkin was unable to communicate with the driver in a language he could understand.

Because of the traffic, by the time he arrived at the conference, the meeting had just gotten underway. The conferees present were Primo Sokolow, Rome; Miguel Cohen, Buenos Aires; Nigel Schwartz, London; Pierre Isaacs, Paris; Shlomo Abrahams, Tel Aviv; Irving

Cohen, Miami; Louis Feldman, Dallas; Mark Chernoff, Chicago; and Sonia Norowitz, New York.

Bushkin reached in his briefcase and placed the agenda on the table. Items for discussion were: Resettlement of Israel and the Potential for a New Zionism, The Development of a New Rabbinic Order, The Placing of the Recently Concluded Holocaust, the So-Called "Second" Final Solution, in a Meaningful Context; Biblical and Torah Study, Worldwide Anti-Semitism, and The Jew in Today's World.

As the meeting ensued, Bushkin was astonished at the way Sonia Norowitz dominated the conversation. It wasn't so much what she had to say, but that she had to say something, always the last word, always the verbal trump card.

"What an obnoxious woman," Bushkin thought to himself as she followed speakers with a nasally abrasive "That's obvious," or "We're wasting time," or "Why can't you see my point? Everyone agrees with me."

After two hours of discussion, the group took a break and Sonia approached Bushkin. "You've been awfully quiet," she said to him.

"Quiet," he said astonishingly.

"Yes," she said. "You haven't said a thing."

"Who can get a word in edgewise? You either dominate the conversation or make people feel awkward when they reply. Are you always this way?"

"I didn't realize I was doing that," she replied meekly.

"Well, you are," Bushkin said sharply.

"I'm sorry," she said softly. "I'm not as bad as I must sound. Say, if you're not committed later, maybe we could have lunch together."

"Only if you let me talk long enough to order my food."

"It's a deal," she said, sticking out her right hand.

"Okay," Bushkin said as he shook her hand in a mocking, half-serious, up-and-down fashion.

"Come sit next to me," she said to Bushkin.

He filed in behind Sonia and sat beside her at the large spherical conference table. He found her attractive. She was fair-skinned with long auburn-colored hair. She was nearly the same height as Sasha, but maybe a little taller, and a bit on the zoftig side, but well built and extremely curvaceous. She exploited her sexuality with a tightly cut, figure-hugging dress that had a low neckline. She had a slow, sensual walk--the kind that made men stare--and her eyes were a striking aqua.

When the meeting ensued, the conferees remained in deep discussion on Israeli resettlement.

"Levi, you haven't offered any input," said Shlomo Abrahams, the moderator of the session, as noon approached.

"What I would like to do," said Bushkin, "is to summarize some of the points already made, add some new ones, and put them in a meaningful order.

"Please do," said Abrahams.

"First, if necessary, a bonus could be paid to induce Jews to settle there.

"Second, land could be sold or leased at a rate where it could be farmed or developed to offer a reasonable return.

"Third, the old-style kibbutz should be discouraged in favor of greater emphasis on private land ownership. People tend to maximize production when financial benefits accrue to them directly.

"Fourth, a representative democracy should be continued with less reliance on socialist solutions.

"Fifth, if Israel is able to be repopulated, and the world and its neighbors remain hostile, a system of financial and military aid would likely have to be maintained, such as existed during the majority of the pre-war era. Of course, such aid would be welcomed now.

"Sixth, and most importantly, Israel must survive as a Jewish state and must continue to be recognized as the homeland."

"Your points are well made and cogent," said Abrahams.

"His comments were pretty obvious," interrupted Sonia.

"Must you keep saying that?" said Bushkin as he smacked his palms against the table.

Before Norowitz could respond, Abrahams said, "Now may be a good time to break for lunch. Let's say we return in an hour and a half."

"Are we still on for lunch?" Bushkin asked Sonia.

"Sure. Don't take anything I say personally."

"It's hard not to," he replied.

As the two exited the Metropolitan Building, it began to rain.

"Dammit," said Sonia.

"What's the problem?" asked Bushkin.

"Do you know how hard it is to catch a cab in the rain?"

After waiting impatiently for five minutes and still behind a mother and two children, a cab appeared. After the mother turned to get the hand of her son, who had wandered a few feet away, Sonia yanked Bushkin by the arm as she entered the cab. He followed because she continued to hold his arm tightly.

"Sonia, that wasn't our cab," he told her.

"It is now," she said.

"Forty-sixth Street and Sixth Avenue, Sweeney's Restaurant," she told the driver.

"My God, that was rude," Bushkin told her.

"She would have done it to me if she had the chance," Sonia said.

"What alley were you raised in?" said Bushkin.

"Don't be naive," she said. "I read on your resume that you are a literature professor."

"I am."

"Do you enjoy it?"

"Yes."

"Why?"

"I enjoy reading and interpreting high literary achievement.

"Sonia, I understand you're in advertising."

"Yes, our firm is Norowitz, Overmeade and Welsley. NOW Advertising is our acronym."

"Do they ever call you Two WASPs and a Jew?"

"You're a real wisenheimer, aren't you?"

"Yes, with added emphasis on the 'heimer.' You know you really bring out the 'heimer' in me, so much so that I feel like a 'double-heimer.'"

"I didn't think that was funny."

"I did. Let me guess, in your firm, Sonia, you're the pushy one."

"How did you know?"

"ESP."

"I don't think you like me," she said.

"It's not that I don't like you, I've known you for a little more than two hours and I don't believe I've met anyone quite like you."

"Do you mean that as a compliment?"

"Not exactly."

"Here we are at Sweeney's," she told Bushkin. "I'll pay the cab fare."

"Let me pick it up," he said.

"No, I insist."

"Well, I was told never to argue with a lady. You are a lady, aren't you?"

"Very funny."

As they sat down, the waiter came over to take their order.

"I'll have a hamburger, rare, but not too rare," she said.

"And you, sir, how do you want yours?"

"Edible," Bushkin said.

"That's one hamburger for the lady, rare but not too rare, and one hamburger for the gentleman, edible," the waiter repeated.

"Eat the pickles, Levi, they're good."

"No, I never eat pickles at lunch. They make me feel omniscient. Pretty soon I might be telling speakers 'that's obvious,' or 'we're wasting time,' or 'why can't you see my point? Everyone agrees with me.'"

"You're very subtle, aren't you," Sonia said mockingly.

As Bushkin was about to reply, the waiter brought the food. Sonia bit into her hamburger.

"It's too rare," she told the waiter. "Take it back."

"Yes, ma'am," he said.

As Bushkin bit into his hamburger, the waiter asked, "And how is yours, sir?"

"Edible," he replied.

"You see, ma'am," said the waiter, "we do get the orders right, sometimes."

"Why did I know you were going to send your hamburger back?" said Bushkin.

"Let me guess," said Sonia, "ESP."

"That must be it. I knew we had something in common," Bushkin replied.

"Sonia, when the waiter brings back the hamburger, please no more complaints. I don't want to miss any more of the conference."

"Scout's honor," she said.

The waiter soon brought back the hamburger.

"One hamburger," he said, "rare, but not too rare, and certainly less rare than before."

"No more complaints, Sonia, eat the hamburger," Bushkin snapped. "I didn't come to New York to watch you send back hamburger."

The two finished their meal in silence.

On their way back to their conference in the cab, Sonia said, "Levi, your points on the resettlement of Israel were well made."

"Oh," he said sarcastically, "I thought they were 'pretty obvious.'"

The two said nothing for the remainder of the ride.

Back at the conference, the session on Israeli resettlement was soon concluded.

Shlomo Abrahams said, "Where there was general unanimity, I will summarize the findings and send them out within two weeks after the conference. I will ask for your approval of this section. If the majority approves the section, it will be placed in the larger report, which you will be asked to approve.

"I would like to turn the next phase of the conference over to Levi Bushkin from Ugograd. Levi, in addition to being a professor of literature, is a rabbi to a small congregation."

"Thank you, Shlomo. Before I ask for comments on this afternoon's subject, 'The Development of a New Rabbinic Order,' I will talk to you about my own experience in Ugograd.

"Soon after the Holocaust ended, I found a woman in hiding and we settled in Ugograd and moved in together. An article appeared about us in our newspaper's national edition. Soon, a few survivors followed and moved to the city. At the time of the High Holidays, Dr. Sasha Liebowitz, whom I moved in with, and I decided it would be appropriate to host a service in our apartment. All the survivors who settled in Ugograd were present.

"I became the rabbi, though I never had any formal training. Rather, I imitated what the rabbis, with whom I was familiar, had done, but left room for my own insights and interpretation. On Yom Kippur, as I was conducting the service and asking God for forgiveness, I told the congregation I couldn't do this and walked out. With that, the service ended.

"In retrospect, I was never ashamed of this act, which was spontaneous and reflected my personal indignation of asking for forgiveness following what may have been the worse genocide in the history of man.

"Yet, I still continued as the rabbi. We have our own shul, and we hold services twice a month and held a communal Seder on Passover. During our services I generally make it a point to give a sermon.

"I don't consider myself a spiritual leader and hope a replacement can be found in the next year. On the other hand, I always felt it was important for a rabbi to emerge and a congregation to be formed to serve as a focal point of our community.

"With that, I turn to the committee members for a discussion and recommendation on the development of a new rabbinical order."

Mark Chernoff of Chicago said, "It is important to reactivate or perpetuate the Yeshivas and colleges, with a Jewish identity.

"Top college graduates who wish to become rabbis should be given scholarships that would pay eighty percent of their tuition.

"Rabbinical students, and rabbis for that matter, should be encouraged to continue to interpret Judaism in the context of a modern world with current problems.

"The rabbinical students and rabbis should devote time to the study of modern philosophy, as well as the literature and music of Jewish writers and composers. These individuals, many times, have a unique understanding of us and should be studied. Hence Judaism must continue to evolve and serve us in the light of the difficulties we have all encountered and shall continue to encounter. It must be a source of inspiration and fulfillment, and provide an appropriate frame of reference.

"As the traditional role of the rabbi has been the teacher, it is of paramount importance, of course, that we have the right 'teachers.'"

"Well put, Mark," said Bushkin.

"Pierre Isaacs," asked Bushkin, "what are your feelings?"

"I've been greatly impressed," he said, "with women in the rabbinate. To my mind, they seem to bring a unique sensitivity and perspective to the bemah.

"What I'm saying is that women should be continued to be encouraged in the profession.

"Also, to add to what Mark Chernoff was saying in terms of getting the 'right teachers,' the rabbis should have a clear and distinctive grasp of the secular world."

"Sonia," Bushkin said, "you've been very quiet this session. Do you have anything to say?"

"No," she said meekly.

"I guess that's obvious," he replied. "Let's take a fifteen-minute break," he said.

As they left the conference room, Sonia approached Bushkin in the hall.

"Why did you put me down?" she said.

"You had it coming."

"I did?"

"Yes, you did."

"What are you doing for dinner tonight?" Sonia asked.

"I'll be dining alone."

"How about joining me?"

"Only if I can send the food back this time. It's my turn, you know."

"That's obvious," she said.

"That's my Sonia," he replied.

"We'll go to dinner right from the conference."

"Okay," said Bushkin.

The conference soon ended for the day.

Following the uneventful dinner, Bushkin and Sonia met for breakfast the next morning at the hotel at which Bushkin was staying, the Warwick.

"How did you think the conference went yesterday?" Sonia asked.

"Pretty well. I didn't think any of the comments were in any way remarkable, but the suggestions and conclusions were solid and meaningful . . . about what I expected.

"How about you?"

"I thought pretty much the same," she replied.

"You did," he said astonishingly.

"Yes, very much so, Levi."

"I didn't think you could agree with anything anyone said. I figured no matter what someone said, you had to have the last word."

"I'm not as terrible as you think."

"I didn't say you were terrible, just purposely difficult."

"I can change," she said. "Maybe you can help reprogram me."

"I am not that good a technician, Sonia."

"I think you're better than you think. Besides, I find you attractive and stimulating."

"You do? That's a relief. My students and congregation think otherwise. When I speak, I'm known variously as Dr. Yawn or the Yawn King, sometimes both. I give people their choice."

"Cut the sarcasm, Levi, I don't want to spar with you. I would like to get to know you better."

"It's getting late," Bushkin said uneasily.

"Waiter," he said, "bring the check."

"Yes, sir."

"I'll pay," he said.

"I never argue with a gentleman," she replied.

As he lay the money on the table, Sonia said, "Take my hand."

"Okay."

The two then held hands as they walked to the conference, five blocks away.

As they entered the conference, Nigel Schwartz of London was beginning to moderate a session on "The Placing of the Holocaust, the So-Called 'Second' Final Solution, in a Meaningful Context."

"Levi, your thoughts, please."

His face became ashen, and he paused before he spoke.

After speaking emotionally for ten minutes, Bushkin said, "Needless to say, as you have heard, this is so troubling for me, as it is for all of us. The whole matter of religious genocide is sad, inexplicable and a certification of man's inhumanity to man. Our Jewish history is fraught with genocide: There has been pogrom and holocaust in astonishing proportions.

"Following World War II, we remembered Dachau, Buchenwald and Babi Yar. We said, 'Never again.'

"We had the war-crime trials at Nuremburg. We said, 'Never again.' Our writers, our philosophers, our cinema producers and composers brought us the story, drama and explanation of the Holocaust. And we said, 'Never again.'

"Well, 'Never' has happened again. The demagogues have poisoned the atmosphere against us. They came from nowhere. They gain control. They turn the masses into a mob. And we suffer.

"How can we prevent this? We can write, we can educate, we can tell the inhumanity of our story. But we can only do so much.

"What is the context of all this: random hooliganism and insanity, that is all.

"As the Semitic minority we have to work hard to achieve our goals. Yet it is because of the notoriety of our achievements that we open ourselves up to the assaults of the demagogues and their mobs.

"So where is the context: The disgrace of man's inhumanity to man, that's where."

As Bushkin finished, the panelists sat in silence. Nigel Schwartz, recognizing the atmosphere Bushkin's talk produced, said softly, "Let's take a break."

Some conferees sat, contemplating Bushkin's words. Others got up slowly. Bushkin, filled with rage from his words, left the room immediately upon the announcement of the break. Sonia followed him.

"You were very impressive, Levi," Sonia told him. Full of rage and emotion, Levi walked away from her, unable to speak. She understood his feelings and didn't try to change his mood. He continued to pace, trying to gather himself. She knew not to speak to him. When the meeting reconvened some fifteen minutes later, Bushkin still had not entered. He appeared to be in a trance-like shell. Sonia stayed by him but did not speak.

Finally she noted his mood began to change and his behavior softened.

"Are you all right?" she asked.

"I'm okay, let's go back in, Sonia."

He sat down, quietly, next to her.

Bushkin didn't say anything the rest of the morning, nor did Sonia.

When lunch came, Sonia said, "Will you join me?"

"Of course," he replied.

The two ate in a small restaurant in the building.

"What are you going to have?" she asked him.

"I'm not hungry, just some soup and crackers. How about you?

"Just a sandwich. As a person, you have a lot of depth," Sonia told him.

"I don't know if that's good or bad," he said.

"I think it's pretty endearing, Levi. After the conference let's go to dinner."

"Sure," Bushkin replied.

How did you survive the war, Sonia?"

"I was a colonel's mistress. I was his Jewish concubine."

"I bet you were pretty good."

"If I wasn't," she said matter-of-factly, "I wouldn't be alive. How about you, Levi?"

If the war had lasted another day, I would have been murdered. What do they say: Timing is everything. By a thread of time I lived."

"Levi, in your discussion on developing a new rabbinic order, you mentioned another woman. Are you serious?"

"I was," he said, "but it's over."

"I'm sorry to hear that."

"Are you?"

"In some ways yes and other ways no," she said as she smiled mischievously at him.

He looked into her eyes and returned the smile. The two clasped hands and continued to stare into each other's eyes.

"It's almost a shame we have an afternoon session," she said.

"First things first," he replied.

With that, the two exited and returned to the conference.

During the afternoon session, Miguel Cohen moderated a session on Biblical Judaism and Torah study. As he polled the conferees for their opinion, Sonia said, "This aspect of Judaism is important. The stories of Abraham, Moses, the Egyptian Bondage, King David, and Solomon, among others, are beautiful works, tinged with imperfection and morality, and are fraught with meaning and substance. In many ways they are the basis of our faith and have tremendous moral overtones that can be a guide for modern life.

"Still, it's important that in Jewish study the whole gamut of thought be examined, from the ancient to the modern. With that, the student will likely achieve his greatest perspective."

"Levi," said Cohen, "your thoughts, please."

"Astonishing as it may seem, I actually agree with Sonia."

The conferees laughed hysterically.

"Seriously," he went on, "the Bible and concomitant Torah study are extremely important. However, I think the greatest perspective can be gained when the Biblical can be juxtaposed against the later historical, modern and post-modern Jewish thought and philosophy."

During the afternoon break, Levi said to Sonia, "I was intrigued when you used the word 'morality.' When I first met you I thought your idea of morality was to grab someone else's cab and then scratch their eyes out."

"I told you," she responded, "I wasn't as bad as I sounded."

"On the contrary, Sonia, you have a lot going for you. You're bright, attractive and very assertive."

"Maybe we could have a lot going for us," she replied.

Bushkin didn't respond. After an awkward pause, Sonia said, "Levi, where are we going for dinner tonight?"

"I'm not particular," he said, "some place nice, maybe a steak house."

"Okay," she said, "and how about a play afterwards."

"Fine."

"You know tomorrow is the last day of the conference. When will you be going back to Ugograd?"

"I was going to leave Thursday morning, but I'm having second thoughts. Maybe I'll stay through the weekend and leave Sunday."

"Of everything you've said since I've known you, that's the most agreeable thing I have heard you say."

"That's obvious," he said.

She smiled at him, overjoyed at the prospect of spending extra time with him. He, too, was equally happy. The more he got to know her, the more he wanted to know her. He realized the hard edge of her personality was a camouflage for a bright, engaging, attractive woman.

During the remainder of the afternoon session, neither Sonia nor Levi said anything.

When the session ended she said, "Come back to my apartment with me so I can change."

"Okay," he said.

As they walked back to her apartment, Sonia said, "Where will you be staying when the conference ends?"

"At the hotel."

"I don't think so," she said.

"Oh, where should I stay?"

"Where you'll be staying tonight."

"And where is that?"

"Let me give you a hint: We're on our way there now."

When he heard those words, he stopped Sonia, kissed her passionately as they stood on the sidewalk, and proceeded to her apartment with his arm around her.

They entered her apartment. He sat down in the living room and waited for her to change.

When she emerged from the bedroom, Sonia was in a tight-fitting light green dress with a low back and neckline. She wore pearls.

Her long auburn hair teased its way down her bare back, and the cleavage she displayed titillated him. She then turned around slowly to reveal the flower of her figure.

"My God you're attractive," he said softly.

"Oh," she said innocently.

"If you wear that outfit on the street, you will add to the homeless problem."

Ignoring the joke, she moved closer to him and began to rub her fingernails over his bottom lip. He pushed her hand away.

He said, "If you keep this up, I'm going to defect. Let's save this for later."

She winked.

He said, "I hope the play is short."

She stared intently into his eyes, refusing to blink. She again rubbed his bottom lip with her fingernails.

He picked her up in his arms and carried her to the bedroom. He laid her down on the bed.

He hovered over her and unbuttoned his shirt. He removed his pants. He then ripped her dress off.

Bushkin and Sonia made love.

As he lay in bed with her, staring at the ceiling, he said, "I've been wanting to do this since I really got to know you."

"The feeling is mutual, Levi."

"Let's forget tonight's plans. Why don't we eat in," he said.

"I'm not much of a cook, Levi."

"Well, we can walk outside and grab something fast."

"Like hamburger," she said.

"Hamburger is fine with me, so long as you don't send it back."

"Honest, I'll be on my best behavior."

"You already have," he replied.

The two laughed uncontrollably.

"Let me change again," Sonia said to him.

"Please put on something a little less alluring because I'm hungry . . . I mean for food."

"Okay, Levi."

She came down in jeans and a white sleeveless top.

"You look good in anything," he said.

"Let's go," said Sonia.

"Where?"

"To eat," she replied.

"I guess we'll come back here for dessert."

"But I don't have anything," she protested.

"I didn't mean that kind of dessert."

When the two awoke the next morning Sonia said, "Did you enjoy last night?"

"Yes, that was the best hamburger I ever ate. I must get their recipe."

"I meant the dessert," she said.

"Oh, that. If the hamburger was good, the dessert was out of this world."

The two embraced and began to kiss each other passionately.

"Let me get up," he said. "I have to check out of my hotel. I'll meet you at the coffee shop at the Metropolitan Building for breakfast."

"Who's stopping you from getting up?" she asked.

"I am. Remind me to stop that or I'll stay in bed with you all day."

Bushkin showered and dressed. He went back to the hotel; put on a fresh suit; checked out; and met Sonia at the coffee shop, forty-five minutes prior to the last day of the conference.

As the two had breakfast, bagels and coffee, Sonia asked Bushkin, "What do you think of the conference at this point?"

"It's been interesting. These are difficult times and issues. Hopefully, what comes out of our group can make a difference. But you wonder."

With that, the two went upstairs for the final session of the conference.

As they sat down, Sonia began to moderate the last topics: "World-wide Anti-Semitism" and "The Jew in Today's World."

Originally, the topics were to be discussed individually. Seeing the conferees had grown mentally tired by the third day of intense discussion, Sonia suggested the last two topics be combined. The panelists agreed.

When the resulting conversation yielded none of the spontaneity and promise of the previous two days, she told the members, "The hour grows late. I think we're all tired. Levi, how about you for the last word?"

Unprepared to say anything at that instance, he cleared his throat several times.

He began to speak softly: "Anti-Semitism will always be with us. Hopefully, the violent strains of our historical and recent past can be avoided.

"Maybe 'Never again' will eventually mean 'Never again.' As a people, I think we can cope with anything but the ruthless violence that has beset us.

"To best function in today's world it is for us to understand who we are. Because if we don't, the world will surely remind us of what we are."

"Levi," Sonia said, "you've had the last word."

# Chapter XVII

## More Sonia

It was Thursday, the day after the conference had ended. Sonia had gone into work early. Bushkin planned to meet her for lunch and spend the afternoon and evening with her.

As he lay in her bed, he began to think, as he often had in his few spare moments, about how lucky he had been to survive the Holocaust. Such thoughts made him feel terribly guilty. "I didn't deserve to live any more than my co-religionists deserved to die," he said to himself. "Such a grotesque injustice," he protested out loud.

Too, he began to think about Sasha. It had been a year since they had met. But the promise of the relationship had dissolved. He hoped she was doing well but remained angry at her and blamed her for the breakup.

He decided to shower, shave and take a walk. He loved to walk in the city, especially at night, when the tall buildings were bathed in light, and the traffic and people formed a continual swirl, a visual cacophony that delighted and energized him. After walking several blocks, he decided to take a cab and look at the United Nations building. He got out of the cab at First Avenue and Forty-second Street. He looked upon the structure, which had changed little since the early 1950s. He thought about the UN's mission and failure.

"Noble ideas," he thought to himself. "If only the people could be as noble as the ideals."

After walking around the structure, he decided not to enter, but hailed another cab. This time he went to Times Square and began to walk. His thoughts turned to Sonia, whom he had only met three days ago. Because of the intensity of their relationship, it seemed to him that they had known each other for six months.

Relationships, he found, were far more intense than in the pre-war era. Maybe this was because people were so unsure about the future they poured everything into the moment, as if tomorrow would never come; or was it because people were suddenly thrown together in ways they could never have imagined? To be sure, Bushkin knew the Holocaust had produced awkward times and improbable, if not seemingly impossible, relationships.

In the short time they were together, he had become extremely fond of Sonia. He compared her to Sasha: pretty, intelligent, and a bit more of an alley cat, at least outwardly. But when you got to know her she was a real woman: feminine, sedate and as soft spoken as anyone he had hoped to know. And was she sensual. My God was she ever!

On the other hand, was it feasible to try and have a relationship, as they lived forty-six hundred miles apart. "Don't think about that," he said to himself. "Enjoy a couple of days with her. The future, if it is meant to be, will take care of itself."

His thoughts then turned to the High Holidays, Rosh Hashanah and Yom Kippur, which would occur in the following month, September.

He hoped for a hundred to attend services, a far cry from the year before when there weren't enough Jews in Ugograd to have a minyan. At that point, he began to formulate ideas for a sermon on Yom Kippur. The theme would be "Keeping God in Our Soul." As for Rosh Hashanah, the fact that as many as a hundred could be attending could be used as a metaphor of the hoped-for and eventual world-wide Jewish revival.

On the other hand, an outburt of anti-Semitism in the form of a mob action remained a dangerous possibility, as Father Yosef Vagins had warned him.

Because lunch time was approaching, he walked from Times Square to NOW Advertising, in the Multi-Media Building at Madison Avenue and Fifty-first Street. He arrived at 12:30 as Sonia was leaving a meeting. She appeared very tense.

"What's the matter?" he asked her.

"We're preparing a large presentation for a dominant auto manufacturer on Monday. We're trying to iron out some kinks, and everyone's on edge.

"If we get this account, it will be a tremendous plus for us and our billings will explode."

"What are your chances?"

"Pretty good."

"Are you sure you want to spend the afternoon with me?"

"I'm sure."

"How about Chinese food?" said Sonia.

"Fine."

The couple walked two blocks to the Ming Dynasty. Each had a chicken dish with rice and tea. Following lunch, they decided to tour the Museum of

Modern Art, where Sonia was a member and served on the Planning Committee.

As they toured the upper floors, Bushkin said, "How some of this stuff is considered priceless is beyond me. I could do the same thing with a strainer and a spray can."

"Your name isn't Jackson Pollack," Sonia caustically reminded him.

"At these prices, I'll change my name," he said.

"Let's go back to the apartment and change for dinner. How about a play afterwards?"

"Okay," he said. "What's playing that's worth seeing?"

"I've heard people recommend the <u>Odyssey</u>."

"What's that about?"

"Man's search for eternal truth."

"Just what I needed," Bushkin said. "After grappling, philosophically, for three days with the future of Judaism, I now have to sit through man's search for eternal truth. Great timing," he added sarcastically. "A perfect antidote for three days of heavy intellectual discussion."

"Come on, you'll enjoy it," she said.

"Okay."

"And how about dinner? How about the Cattleman and we'll eat some steak."

"If we order hamburger, remind me, Sonia, whose turn it will be to send it back."

"I can't recall," she quipped.

"Are you enjoying my company, Levi?"

"Remarkably so."

"That's how I feel about being with you, Levi."

"Let's keep enjoying ourselves for the time remaining. Let me go in and change. I won't be too long," he said.

Fifteen minutes later, he returned in a charcoal-gray suit with a cloud-white shirt and a raging crimson tie with barely perceptible white rings.

"Are you going to change?" he asked.

"I'm going to freshen up."

"Don't be too long."

"I never keep a gentleman waiting."

As they walked to the Cattleman, the couple projected an aura of extreme good looks combined with dignity and grace. Some onlookers stared at them; others made contact from the corners of their eye.

They entered the restaurant and were seated promptly.

"How involved were you with that woman from Ugograd?" she asked.

"I don't want to talk about it," he said.

"Why?"

"Because I'm human, that's why."

At that moment, the waiter brought the menus.

"What's good?" he asked Sonia.

"Try the filet mignon."

"And what will you have, Sonia?"

"The same. When the waiter returns, order for both of us."

"Sure."

The waiter returned and Bushkin placed the order for filet mignon and a red wine, which was soon brought over.

After the wine was poured, Sonia made a toast.

"To us," she said.

Bushkin nodded his approval and the two clicked their glasses and drank.

"I'd like to now propose a toast," said Bushkin.

"What's that?" said Sonia.

"Here's to eternal hope for our people."

"And to our happiness," she added.

The two again perfunctorily clicked their glasses and drank.

"Take my hand," she told him.

He did and then began to rub her palm in a circular motion with his middle finger.

"That feels good. Will you be having dessert tonight?" she asked him.

"Where?"

"In the apartment," she said.

"Of course, I can get hooked on that."

She laughed and his laughter parroted hers.

"You know, Levi, you're very stimulating."

"How so?"

"In every way I need."

The couple now laughed in unison.

"Are you looking forward to the fall semester?"

"I suppose."

"You know with your aptitude for literature, you ought to consider writing."

"I've begun to think about it."

"What would you write about?"

"Likely a Jewish theme, there enough of them."

"I'd bet you'd be a very compelling story-teller."

"Thank you. And who knows," he said, "with my aptitude for religion maybe I'll become God."

"And then what would you do?"

"Our people would never be the victims of Holocaust."

"Amen," she said.

With that, the food was served. As Sonia took a bite of her filet, Bushkin asked her how her meal was.

When she said "fine," Bushkin put his napkin to his brow, pretending to mop the sweat caused from the tension of whether Sonia would send back her food.

Laughing hysterically, she asked Bushkin, "How is yours?"

"Fine," he said. "I'm easy to please."

"I could tell that last night," she said.

"When was that?"

"During dessert in my apartment." He laughed uncontrollably.

The two said little during the remainder of the meal but stared at each other lovingly and incessantly.

When it was time to order dessert, Sonia asked him, "Here or in the apartment?"

"I think we will go with the logical order of sequence tonight," said Bushkin in a polished professorial tone.

"Dammit," said Sonia mockingly. "I liked last night's order better."

"To tell you the truth, I did too, but tonight this dessert before that dessert."

"I see," Sonia said, feigning disappointment.

"What's good for this dessert, Sonia?"

"Try the apple pie."

"Will it be as good as the dessert we will have later?"

"Nothing is that good," she said.

When the waiter approached the table, Bushkin told him, "Two pieces of apple pie, two coffees, and a check, please."

As the two ate their dessert, Sonia said, "Levi, Sunday will be here soon. Is it possible we'll have a future together?" Bushkin didn't answer.

Following the meal, the couple took a cab to the theatre to see the Odyssey. During the performance, Sonia intermittently rested her head on his shoulder and held his hand, almost throughout the entire performance. She noticed how intense he became as the plot evolved. She found it interesting that his mood could evolve from one of comedic banter to riveting intensity in such a short time.

As they exited the play, she asked him what he thought.

"Man's search for meaning," he scoffed. "One of the eternal questions. Some people find it in religion, others in vegetarianism, others in anti-Semitism. I guess I'm too cynical of a critic. Besides, I thought the plot was predictable, the characters boring, and the dialogue was an endless stream of cliches. That said, if someone asks you to invest in this play, you should. Because if I think it's barely mediocre, the play will likely run for twenty years, make a lot of money and be on everyone's must-see list."

In the cab on the way home, Sonia repeated to him, "Do we have a future together?"

"We live forty-six hundred miles apart. Who is going to move?" he replied.

"If we give ourselves a chance, things can work out."

Bushkin remained silent.

As they entered the apartment, she turned and hugged him passionately. "I've never enjoyed four days more than I have with you," she told him lovingly.

"I feel the same, Sonia."

The two soon went to bed.

When they awoke the next morning, Friday, Sonia told him, "I will go to the office in the morning. Meet me for lunch, and we will spend the afternoon together."

"Fine," he said, "I'm going to sleep a little longer."

"Pleasant dreams."

"They will be if I'm dreaming of you."

At 12:30 p.m., he met her at the office. "How is the presentation coming?" he asked.

"We'll be ready. After you leave Sunday, we will be in the office for another run through. We are very confident at this point."

"Come Sunday I will miss you terribly."

"The feeling is mutual," she said.

"Where should we go to lunch?"

"How about Little Italy?"

"Fine."

As they exited the cab on Mulberry Street, Sonia and Bushkin began looking for a restaurant.

They stopped at Roma's and read the menu in the window.

"Let's go in," Bushkin said. The couple was seated near a window that overlooked the street.

"What will you have?" asked Sonia.

"Antipasto, veal parmigiana and red wine."

"I'll have the same," she said. "Order for me when the waiter comes."

"Certainly."

Bushkin placed the order.

Sonia asked during lunch, "What will we do tonight?"

"How about seeing the Gershwin revival," Bushkin said.

"Perfect," said Sonia.

"Anyway," Bushkin said, "I'd rather hear a genius's music than watch some lousy play."

"Whatever you want," she said.

"If you're not happy, Sonia, let me know and we'll do what you want."

"No, Gershwin and Bushkin are a great combination."

"'NOW' that's good copywriting, a slogan worth remembering. 'NOW' I know why you're in advertising."

"You're a sly punster," said Sonia as she got up and performed a mock curtsy. Bushkin applauded.

Following lunch the two walked, window shopped and talked about a political bribery scandal occurring in New York.

As they approached Canal Street, she asked him, "What are your hopes for the future?"

"Happiness, peace and prosperity."

"With whom?"

"I'm not sure. How about you?"

"Same hopes: happiness, peace and prosperity."

"With whom?"

"Some literature professor I met on Monday."

"Sonia, living forty-six hundred miles apart, how are we going to work this out?"

"Where there's a will, there's a way."

"You still haven't answered my question: How are we going to work this out? Are you going to move to Ugograd?"

"How about moving to New York?"

"I can't pick up and go. I have a job, a congregation and responsibility. A courtship will be difficult."

"Do we need one?"

"Yes."

"Maybe we can meet for extended periods on holidays or grab some long weekends in London."

"Anything is possible. Do we have to talk about this now?"

"When should we talk about this? You'll be leaving Sunday."

"Maybe we shouldn't talk about it. Let's let things happen. If we're meant to be, we're meant to be."

"But, Levi, why shouldn't we talk about it?"

"Okay, we'll talk. But do you have an answer?"

"Only that I love being with you."

"I feel the same."

"I still think you have a lot of feeling for Sasha."

"How did you know her name?"

"You mentioned her during the conference."

"You must have been paying very close attention."

"I was."

"I told you I still had feelings for her. I repeat, I'm only human."

"I think it's deeper than that. I think you're still deeply in love with her."

"I don't think so."

"I think there is something holding you back from me, and it's her."

"I don't think so. Can't we enjoy ourselves?"

"I want to talk about this."

"I don't."

"I do."

"Look, I'm not going to love someone who doesn't love me."

"That's easier said than done."

"Are you in advertising or psychoanalysis?"

"You're an easy read."

"Don't be so sure."

"I'm sure."

"Please, I feel like I'm being interrogated."

"I'm sorry."

"Look, Sonia, if we're meant to be, we're meant to be. You're making me feel uncomfortable."

"I'm sorry, but I want this to go further than this week."

"I do too."

He then grabbed her and kissed her passionately.

"I'm looking forward to tonight," he said.

"I am too."

"Let's take a cab back, Sonia. Both of us could use some rest."

Bushkin hailed a cab. Inside the cab, Bushkin said, "I don't think I'll be hungry for dinner. A sandwich is fine with me."

"I feel the same; that was a heavy lunch."

When they got back to Sonia's apartment, she said, "Tomorrow will be our last full day together."

"That makes me sad," he said. "You know I've just spent the best week of my life, with you."

"I feel the same. Come here."

He walked over to her and began to hug and kiss her with great feeling. "You're terrific. You're beautiful. I love you," he said.

"Stay in this country, Levi."

"I can't. I have to go back. We can work this out if we try."

"Don't go back. I know if you go back I will lose you."

"We can work it out," he repeated.

He then picked her up in his arms and took her to the bedroom.

As he laid her down in the bed, she said, "Make love to me. I want to be with you. Don't leave me."

# Chapter XVIII

## The Old World Beckons

The sun had not yet risen to splash the city in light. It was early Sunday morning, and Bushkin was finishing packing. Sonia awoke.

"Can't you stay longer?" she asked him.

"I can't. I really have to get back."

She remained silent as he finished packing.

As he closed his last bag, she said she would get dressed and ride with him to Newark Airport.

"Don't be too long," he said.

"I won't, Levi."

When she emerged in bright-red slacks and a tight-fitting white top that paid perfect homage to her curvaceous figure, he said, "It's too early for you to look so sinfully good. I must be crazy to leave this."

"My point exactly. Stay," she commanded.

"I can't. Call the cab, please."

"I'm not going to dial the number."

"Okay, I will."

After he did, Bushkin said, "The cab will be here in fifteen minutes."

"You son-of-a-bitch," she said. "You bastard."

"Stop it."

"No."

"Maybe it's best of you don't go to the airport."

"I'm going."

"Then no more outbursts."

Sonia began to pout.

"Snap out of it," he said. "I feel terrible, too."

"Hold me," she said.

As he put his arms around her, she said, "Don't let me go."

"Let's go downstairs to wait for the cab," he said.

"On second thought, maybe you should go to the airport without me."

"Okay."

"Wait a second, let me help you with your bags."

"That won't be necessary."

"I said I will help you. I don't want you to make a second trip."

"Then help with these two suit bags. Are you sure they're not too heavy?"

"I'm sure."

As they waited outside for the cab, he said, "Are you going with me to the airport?"

"No," she said.

"Well, then, we'll say good-bye here."

"I changed my mind."

"What's gotten into you, Sonia? You're acting like a child."

He put his arms around her and began to caress her softly.

"Don't stop that," she said.

The cab came. When it stopped she got in and slammed the door.

"What's her problem, mister?" said the driver.

"You'll have to ask her."

"Never mind, I got my own problems."

"Don't we all," replied Bushkin.

As the car began to pull away from the curb, Sonia began to seethe.

"Now what's the problem?" Bushkin asked her.

"Don't you know?"

"What should I do?"

"Stay."

"If I could, I would."

"You could."

"Driver," said Bushkin, "pull over and let her out."

As he began pulling over, Sonia said, "I'm sorry, Levi. I just didn't want this day to come."

She embraced him and he kissed her passionately, as the cab was now parked at the curb.

"Mister," said the driver as they held their embrace, "is she staying or going?"

"I'm staying," said Sonia, "continue on to the airport."

As the cab pulled out in traffic, she said, "Levi, when can we see each other again?"

"How about during your Thanksgiving and during my Christmas recess," he answered.

"I'd look forward to that. And maybe I'll surprise you at another time."

"Oh," he said.

"I want to work this out. I'm very determined to make this happen," she said.

"Don't force things, Sonia, let things evolve. Be natural. Be yourself."

"I am."

"Maybe you're attracted to me because in your mind you know you can't have me," Bushkin said.

"That's not it."

"Are you sure?"

"I adored the time we spent together. The things we did. The repartee and the love-making."

"I feel the same," he said.

When the driver pulled into the airport, Bushkin asked her if she would wait until he boarded.

"Certainly," she said.

He reported to his gate and then went with Sonia for some coffee.

"I see the plane's on time," she said.

"Yes," he answered.

"Our relationship is going to be okay," he continued.

"I know so," she replied.

When his plane was announced for boarding, he approached the ramp.

"I guess this is it for a while," he said.

"We don't have a choice," she replied.

They embraced and kissed lovingly.

"Be faithful to me, Levi."

"And you do the same, Sonia."

"I love you, Levi."

"I love you too, Sonia."

He began to walk down the ramp. Bushkin had tears in his eyes, as she did.

As he got into his seat, Bushkin fastened his seatbelt, put his head back, and began to think. His mind was restless, and he asked the flight attendant to bring him some paper and a pen. He began to compose a letter.

My Dearest Sonia,

I've only known you for a short time, but I feel I've known you for so very long.

Our week together was fantastic. I enjoyed everything about you.

As I write this, the plane is readying for take-off. I want you to know I will do everything in my power to make this relationship work.

I love you and look forward to seeing you as soon as is humanly possible.

My Love to You Always,
Levi

With the plane over the Atlantic, Bushkin tilted his seat back and closed his eyes.

He was soon asleep and began to dream. He was delivering a sermon on Yom Kippur. Unlike last year, he was at ease and not conflicted about asking God for forgiveness so soon after the Holocaust.

Suddenly the doors of the synagogue swing open. It was the police. They raced up to the bemah and grabbed him.

"Get off me," he said.

"We're taking you away."

"Why?"

"The war is not over. You're going back to the death camp."

Two held him by his arms.

As they escorted him outside the building, he saw an open field and woods just beyond. He broke loose from his captors and ran towards the woods. He was fifty yards away when two police dogs latched on to him. One had him by the arm and the other by the leg. The police were soon over him and shackled his arms and legs.

"Shall we kill the Jew here?" one said.

"Our orders are to take him to the death camp," another replied.

As they stood him up, Bushkin began to scream.

"Are you okay, mister?" said the passenger sitting beside him.

"What. What. What," Bushkin said groggily.

"Are you okay?" the passenger repeated.

"I must have been dreaming," said Bushkin slowly. "It all seemed so real."

"You were screaming," said the passenger.

"I was?"

"Yeah, and very loud. And your face is covered with sweat."

Seeing a Mezuzah hanging out of Bushkin's shirt, the passenger said, "Say, mister, are you a Jew?"

"Yes. Why do you ask?"

"Because if I were a Jew, I'd scream too."

Bushkin unbuckled his seatbelt and went to the men's room to freshen up.

He sat down, tilted his head back, and began to recall a part from Philip Roth's <u>Portnoy's Complaint</u> that always made him laugh uproariously. He liked to think of this passage when he wanted to lighten his mood. As the acting rabbi of his congregation, he particularly liked to recall the segment when the fourteen-year-old Alexander Portnoy says:

"But I am something more, or so they tell me. A Jew. No! No! An *atheist*, I cry. I am nothing where religion is concerned, and I will not pretend to be anything that I am not! I don't care how lonely and needy my father is, the truth about me is the truth about me, and I'm sorry but he'll just have to swallow my apostasy whole! And I don't care how close we

176

came to sitting *shiva* for my mother either--actually, I wonder now if maybe the whole hysterectomy has not been dramatized into C-A and out of it again solely for the sake of scaring the S-H out of me! Solely for the sake of humbling and frightening me into being once again an obedient and helpless little boy! And I find no argument for the existence of God, or for the benevolence and virtue of the Jews, in the fact that the most re-ver-ed man in all of Newark came to sit for "a whole half hour" beside my mother's bed. If he emptied her bedpan, if he fed her her meals, that might be the beginning of something, but to come for half an hour and sit beside a bed? What else has he got to do, Mother? To him, uttering beautiful banalities to people scared out of their wits--that is to him what playing baseball is to me! He loves it! And who wouldn't? Mother, Rabbi Warshaw is a fat, pompous, impatient fraud, with an absolutely grotesque superiority complex, a character out of Dickens is what he is, someone who if you stood next to him on the bus and didn't know he was so revered, you would say, "That man stinks to high heaven of cigarettes," and that is *all* you would say. This is a man who somewhere along the line got the idea that the basic unit of meaning in the English language is the syllable. So no word he pronounces has less than three of them, not even the word *God*. You should hear the song and dance he makes out of *Israel*. For him it's as long as refrigerator! And do you remember him at my bar mitzvah, what a field day he had with Alexander Portnoy? Why, Mother, did he keep calling me by my whole name? Why, except to impress all you idiots in the audience with all those syllables! And it worked! It actually

177

worked! Don't you understand, the synagogue is how he earns his living, *and that's all there is to it*. Coming to the hospital to be brilliant about life (syllable by syllable) to people who are shaking in their pajamas about death is his business, just as it is my father's business to sell life insurance! It is what they each do to earn a living, and if you want to feel pious about somebody, feel pious about my father, God damn it, and bow down to him the way you bow down to that big fat comical son of a bitch, because my father *really* works his balls off and doesn't happen to think that he is God's special assistant into the bargain. And doesn't speak in those fucking *syllables!* "I-a wan-tt to-a wel-come-a you-ew tooo thee sy-no-gawg-a." Oh God, Oh, Guh-ah-duh, if you're up there shining down your countenance, why not spare us from here on out the enunciation of the rabbis! Why not spare us the rabbis themselves! Look, why not spare us religion, if only in the name of our human dignity! Good Christ, Mother, the whole world knows already, *so why don't you? Religion is the opiate of the people!* And if believing that makes me a fourteen-year-old Communist, then that's what I am, *and I'm proud of it!"*

Bushkin also liked to recall the passage, because it helped prevent him from becoming too full of himself and being carried away by what he perceived as his own omnipotence.

As the plane approached the Ugograd Airport, he held the letter addressed to Sonia tightly in his right hand. He asked himself: "Under what circumstances would I not want to mail this letter?"

"There are none," he thought. As Bushkin disembarked from the aircraft, he carefully placed the letter in a mailbox.

Sasha returned to work eight days later, on Monday. "You look beautiful," said Nadia Pavel, her assistant. "Your tan is exquisite. How was your cruise?"

"It was two weeks of the most miserable goddamn boredom I've ever been party to. I hated the goddamn boat. I can't stand that pompous ass, Vasily Ginsberg. I'm getting out of this goddamn relationship."

"When?"

"I will start attending services with the High Holidays. Levi will notice me. After that I will approach him and try for a reconciliation."

"Suppose he refuses?"

"He won't."

"Why are you so sure?"

"Because we love each other, that's why."

"I hope you're right."

"I better be."

On Wednesday night, Levi met with his board of directors to discuss the preparations for the High Holidays. All directors were present with the exception of Vasily Ginsberg and Sasha. Prior to the meeting, he told Yakov Potemkin and Amos Sephard about Sonia. They were astonished to hear how quickly the relationship had blossomed.

They asked him if he had heard from Sasha. "No," he said sharply.

"Do you think about her?" asked Sephard.

"Absolutely not," he replied.

"Whom are you kidding?" said Sephard.

He then looked at Sephard icily.

Despite his protestations to the contrary, both Sephard and Potemkin knew that Sasha remained in his thoughts.

Bushkin then began the meeting. "How many can we expect for Rosh Hashanah and Yom Kippur?" he asked the directors.

"One hundred per service," said Isadore Samonovich.

"I assume all present have reviewed the recommendations on the formal dues' structure, crafted by me, Yakov and Isadore Samonovich," said Bushkin. "Any comments, suggestions or possible amendments?"

"Okay, all in favor of the new dues' structure raise your hand.

"The motion is carried unanimously.

"Tatyana, please advise the members by mail of the new payment structure."

"Certainly, Levi," she replied.

"I want to remind you that--and Tatyana please put in your mailing--contributions will still be encouraged.

"Since all of the promised contributions are in from the original members, with the exception of Vasily Ginsberg, Yakov, please remind Mr. Ginsberg of his pledge from last year when he said he would donate fifty percent more than the highest contribution."

"I will," he said.

"Yakov, I'll wager a week's pay you'll never see a nickel."

"You're on, Levi."

"Then the terms of the bet are this: You'll have sixty days to collect his pledge."

"In that case," said Yakov, "the bet is off."

The directors began to laugh hysterically in unison.

The day after the directors' meeting, Bushkin had arranged to meet Sarah Potemkin at a jewelry shop to help him pick out something appropriate for Sonia. They looked at a gold heart with a line of gems down the center. The beginning letter of each stone spelled out "Dearest."

As they examined the piece, he turned to Sarah and said, "This is perfect. This is exactly what I want."

"You must be extremely fond of her."

"Very much so."

After he purchased the piece, he sent the following note with it:

Dearest Sonia,
Wear this always.
Love, Levi

Sonia received the piece and decided she would spend Yom Kippur in Ugograd.

# Chapter XIX

# Rosh Hashanah, The Jewish New Year

Bushkin went through his mail. A large envelope came from Sonia. He opened it quickly. It was a New Year's card.

It had the following message:

Received your heart. It is so beautiful and yet the thought was more beautiful than the jewelry.

Love you.

L'Shanah Tovah

Bushkin was elated with her words.

A few days later, on the morning of Rosh Hashanah, Sasha awoke and dressed for shul. Vasily Ginsberg would pick her up and they would attend services together.

When his limousine came, she was waiting outside her apartment. His chauffeur stopped and opened the door for her. She got in and sat in the rear seat next to him.

"Happy New Year, darling," Vasily said as she entered and kissed her lightly on the cheek.

"Happy New Year, Vasily."

As they drove to the shul, she felt awkward. She was determined to end the relationship with him and renew her union with Bushkin, whom she hadn't seen since the eve of Passover, some five and a half months ago.

"Darling," said Ginsberg, "you look agitated this morning. But," he continued, "you're still so beautiful."

"Thank you," she said in an unfeeling, matter-of-fact, perfunctory tone.

"My public offering will soon be on the street. I stand to make a small fortune from the sale of the shares."

"Oh," she said. "How many people do you intend to screw this time?"

"Pardon me?" he said.

"You heard me."

"Do you want to be with me?" he asked.

"Not particularly."

"I can arrange that," he said.

"Why don't you?"

"Never mind," he said.

As the chauffeur pulled in front of the shul and let them out, Ginsberg took her hand as they entered.

"Always on stage, aren't you, Vasily?" she said.

He smiled at the congregants as they sat down.

Once seated, she said, "Let's move closer and sit with the Potemkins, Samonoviches, Amos Sephard and Tatyana Samuelson."

"Let's sit here," he replied.

"I'm going to sit with them. If you don't wish to move, you can sit alone."

As she got up, he followed. When he reached for her hand, she brushed it away. When they sat in the desired row, Sasha greeted the Potemkins and their children, the Samonoviches, Amos Sephard and Tatyana Samuelson with a hug and kiss on the cheek. "L'Shanah Tovah," she told each of them. Ginsberg followed in her stead.

Bushkin soon appeared. As he looked over the audience, he was elated the attendance was approximately a hundred. His eyes turned to the row containing the Potemkins. Bushkin's eyes then raced over the row until they met Sasha's. He became temporarily unnerved and dropped his prayer book. As he went to pick it up, he accidentally bumped his head on the lectern. The congregants laughed subduedly among themselves.

Because he had seen Sasha, his thoughts and feelings were isolated on her, and he didn't hear the laughter. As the service was about to begin, he began to stare at her. She stared back. It was almost as if they were alone in the room.

He took his eyes off her and began to fumble through the prayer book. He momentarily forgot where to start the service, and the normally self-assured Bushkin began to stammer as he finally began the morning worship. Sasha knew the reason and felt buoyed by his reaction.

As he went through the service, which included the Shema, Barechu, Shehecheyanu, Aleinu, Kaddish, a prayer for the restoration of Israel, a reference to the Shofar, and a Torah portion that chronicled the story of Abraham and the beginnings of Judaism, Bushkin, after each segment, looked at Sasha. Throughout the service she had not taken her eyes off him. To Sasha, it reminded her of when they met and fell in love. And how, in the beginning, they needed, supported and loved each other. In turn, he was elated to look at her: the beauty, her poise and manner. It was all there as he remembered it, prior to the breakup.

When Bushkin gave his sermon, he began to speak of renewal. As he mentioned the word "renewal," he looked up from his prepared script and stared at Sasha. She felt an immense excitement and optimism for reconciliation.

As he concluded his sermon he said, "Last year we held a service on Rosh Hashanah in 'our' apartment." Again he looked up from his script and his eyes met hers. He then returned to the script. "It was soon after the war, and we didn't have enough people for a minyan.

"Now, fortunately, we are some one hundred strong and we have our own shul. This is progress. Grudging progress, but progress, nonetheless.

"Today we also meet in comparative safety and freedom. This, too, is progress and something that couldn't have been contemplated eighteen months ago.

"History has taught us that progress and renewal are difficult processes." Again, as he said the word "renewal," he looked up from his script and stared at Sasha. She stared back and then they began to smile at each other. Their conduct wasn't lost on the people in their row who knew them best.

"He's telling you he loves you," Yetta Samonovich whispered to Sasha.

"I hope so," she replied.

"Life is not an easy process," Bushkin said, staring at Sasha.

"Decisions are difficult. As we recall the beginnings of Judaism and Abraham's intended sacrifice of Isaac, we know of the impossibility of his choice. This was Abraham's greatest test of faith and obedience, when God commanded him to sacrifice his son, Isaac. Abraham took his son to the mountaintop, laid him on an alter, and prepared to kill him. God intervened, stopped the killing and provided a ram for sacrifice.

"Our faith was then able to continue with Abraham's progeny, Isaac. Yet Judaism, as we know, has had its horrific difficulties--Holocaust, Inquisition and Pogrom. Nonetheless, we are here today, the few and the faithful, as we celebrate our renewal and revival on another New Year. And we do so optimistically, in God's house. May we be part of Judaism's world-wide renewal. May our small congregation serve as a symbol of faith and determination. And then may our people be fruitful and multiply.

"L'Shanah Tovah.

"Amen."

Bushkin paused, giving his congregants, in general, and Sasha, in particular, a chance to contemplate his words and gestures.

Following the sermon, Bushkin made several announcements, the most significant of which was that in approximately six weeks the congregation would be celebrating the one-year anniversary since it moved to its synagogue. "You will soon be advised of the date," he told the congregation.

He then said, "The service will conclude with Adon Olam." After it was sung, Bushkin came down from the bemah to greet the congregants. A line formed in front of him, and he greeted them individually. Soon Sasha appeared in front of him. Neither said a word. She grabbed him and began to hug him. He reciprocated. They held this pose, delighted, once again, to be in each other's arms. She stepped back. "How is my favorite rabbi?" she asked.

"Couldn't be better, Dr. Liebowitz," he replied.

"Don't be a stranger," she said.

"Oh," he replied. And after a pause, he said, "L'Shanah Tovah, Dr. Liebowitz."

He then greeted Yakov and Sarah Potemkin.

The next day Sasha and her assistant, Nadia Pavel, were having morning coffee.

"Did you see Levi yesterday?" Nadia asked.

"Yes."

"How did it go?"

"It's hard to say."

"What do you mean?"

"Well, Nadia, he gave a sermon and in it a key word was 'renewal.' And each time he said it, I had the feeling he and I were alone in the room, staring at each other, and he was talking to me."

"In a way," Nadia replied, "he probably was."

"But at the end of the service when he greeted the congregants, we saw each other, hugged and then he seemed indifferent to me."

"What did he do?"

"I asked him, 'How is my favorite rabbi?' He said, 'Couldn't be better, Dr. Liebowitz.' I told him 'Don't be a stranger.' He said, 'L'Shanah Tovah,' happy New Year in Hebrew. That was it."

"Do you think he's seeing someone else?"

"I doubt it. We're a small community, and I probably would have heard."

"Are you sure?"

"I can't be sure."

"When will you see him again?"

"Yom Kippur, next week."

"Do you know what you're going to do?"

"Following the service, when the congregants greet the rabbi, I will slip a note to him, saying I want to get back together."

Meanwhile, Sonia was completing her plans to surprise Bushkin and be with him on Yom Kippur.

# Chapter XX

## Yom Kippur with Sonia

Bushkin sat in his office. Yom Kippur, the Jewish day of atonement, was to begin that evening at sundown.

There was a knock on the door.

"Come in," he said.

The door opened. He was startled to see Sonia. She was wearing the heart he gave her. They embraced and then kissed lovingly. She sat down, as did he. He became dumbfounded and silent.

"Can't you say anything?" she asked.

"Ya, Ya, Ya, Ya, Ya, Yes," he stammered. He then paused again and was finally able to say, "You, You, You look beautiful. This is an undeserved reward and the best surprise I've ever had. Where are your bags?"

"I had them taken to your apartment."

"How long are you staying?"

"Through Yom Kippur and a day or two afterwards."

"I can't tell you how wonderful it is to see you. I love you."

"Ditto," she said.

"Tonight I'm going to have dinner with Isadore and Yetta Samonovich. Let me call them to set an extra plate."

"I'd like to meet them. Are you sure I won't be an imposition?"

"Not at all. I'll tell them you're a light eater."

She laughed.

As he dialed the phone, he smiled at her giddily.

"Yetta," he said, "I'm bringing a guest for dinner."

"Let me guess. It's Sasha. You have gotten back together. Isn't that wonderful. I knew you two were meant for each other."

"No, no, no," he said, embarrassed, "it's Sonia Norowitz, the woman I met in New York during the World Jewish Congress."

"Oh," she replied. "You must be serious."

"Well, yes," he said.

After he hung up, he asked Sonia to have lunch with him and advised her he had a 2 p.m. class.

"What will you be lecturing on?" she asked.

"<u>Death of a Salesman</u>."

"Poor Willy Loman," Sonia said.

"Yep," Bushkin replied, "poor Willy Loman."

"What will be the basis of your class today?"

"Sustenance and destruction in delusion."

"I would be interested to hear how you handle that."

"You can sit and suffer with the rest of the class."

"I'd love to, I think. Say, that theme doesn't apply to us, does it?"

"Come here, gorgeous," he said.

Bushkin gave her a reassuring hug and then caressed her gently on the back and face.

"Don't stop," she said.

"I wish I didn't have to, Sonia."

When they returned from lunch, they sat in his office and chatted until it was time to go to class.

The two got up and proceeded to a large, unimposing classroom. Sonia took a seat among the students.

Bushkin began a discussion. "By now you should have finished <u>Death of a Salesman</u>. The question for this class today is: Did Willy Loman's delusions that at first sustained him, eventually kill him?

"Igor," said Bushkin, "your comments."

"Willy Loman was an expendable commodity, an aging salesman who wasn't cutting it. Yet, in a sense, he was sustained by a vision, the one of Dave Singleman who was selling into his eighties. And when he died, he was, according to Loman, given a hero's funeral. This was probably an exaggeration.

"After he relates the Singleman story to his boss, Howard, he says, 'There was respect, and comradeship, and gratitude in it. Today, it's all cut and dried, and there's no chance for bringing friendship to bear--or personality. You see what I mean? They don't know me any more.'"

"In other words, Igor, selling was never the exalted profession that Loman made it out to be. Rather, it was produce or be replaced."

"That's right."

"Can you cite another example?"

"Yes. When Willy tells Happy and Biff that when he'll take them--his children--to New England, and says, 'I have friends. I can park my car in any street in New England, and the cops protect it like their own.'

"Willy Loman continually exaggerates his importance."

"Give me one final example."

"Perhaps the saddest episode--the ultimate exclamation point--is the funeral. When Linda, his wife, says, 'Why didn't anybody come?'

"She goes on to say, 'I can't understand it. At this time especially. First time in thirty-five years we were just about free and clear.'"

"Alexei, how would you interpret Willy Loman's suicide?"

"After Willy was fired by Howard and he no longer was a salesman, his life, literally, had ended. If Willy couldn't be who he thought he was--not who he was--he didn't want to live. Hence, to me, Willy's suicide marked the 'death' of a dream and the end of his delusions in a way that transcends the play."

"Very good," said Bushkin. "Two weeks from today I want you to give me a double-spaced, typewritten paper on Willy Loman and his delusions. The topic will be 'Did Delusions Sustain and/or Destroy Him?' The paper will be no shorter than five pages and no longer than ten. Your comments today were impressive. You grasped the material in context and meaning. I expect the same effort in your written material. Class dismissed."

Sonia walked to the lectern.

"Your students respond to you," she said. "That was a nice interaction. They like and respect you."

"Sure, until I give a bad grade," quipped Bushkin. "Let's walk back to my apartment. We'll relax and change for dinner."

At 5:30 p.m., they came to the home of Isadore and Yetta Samonovich. After the introductions and some pleasant conversation, dinner was served.

"I'd like to propose a toast," said Isadore. "May our Jewish community and our Jewish brethren worldwide prosper and may our fast be an easy one on our Day of Atonement."

"Here, here," said Bushkin.

The four clicked their glasses and drank the wine.

As Yetta served dinner, Isadore asked, "Sonia, what do you do?"

"I'm in advertising."

"A tough racket," said Isadore.

"Sonia's firm, NOW Advertising," said Bushkin, "recently got a large contract with an auto manufacturer."

"Yes," interrupted Sonia, "our billings should increase tenfold."

"Mazel tov," said Isadore.

"And what do you do, Isadore?"

"I'm in retailing."

"Also a tough racket," she said.

"It's a business for meshugenas."

"I'm glad you said that. I've been thinking that for years," laughed Yetta.

"What kind of merchandise do you handle?" asked Sonia.

"We're promotional. Fashion-wise, nobody can touch us. We get the best labels, including Paris imports, and nobody, I mean nobody, beats us on price.

"We reopen the day after tomorrow. You'll come in and look. Nobody beats our deals."

"I can get a deal in New York," responded Sonia.

"I'll not only give you a deal, but a 'deal, deal.'"

"You've got a 'deal,'" laughed Sonia. "I'll be there to look over your 'deal, deals.'"

"You know," quipped Bushkin, "if Moses would have come down from Mt. Sinai with an extra set of tablets, the eleventh commandment, undoubtedly, would have said, 'Thou shall not buy retail.'"

"Knowing our people," said Sonia, "it would have probably been commandments eleven through twenty."

Following dinner, as Yetta showed Sonia through the house, Bushkin and Isadore talked in the den.

"She's terrific," said Isadore.

"Who?"

"Who? Whom do you think? Sonia."

"I agree."

"Now I know why it's serious."

"I'm not going to rush into anything. This business of an intercontinental relationship makes things awkward, but I told her we can work it out. When I met her in New York, I was so taken with her that I was tempted to stay. She'll be back on the American holiday of Thanksgiving, and I'm going to New York between Christmas day and New Year's."

"Does Sasha know about her?"

"Not unless someone has told her."

At that moment, Yetta and Sonia returned.

"You have a beautiful home, Isadore," said Sonia.

"Thank you."

"Let's go back to the dining room for dessert," said Yetta.

At the mention of the word 'dessert,' Sonia and Bushkin began to laugh hysterically.

"I'm sorry," said Sonia, "it's an inside joke."

"I understand," said Isadore, smiling.

During dessert, Isadore said, "Levi, I want to thank you for what you've done for our community. You've been a pillar of strength and, in a way, the anchor we needed. Words can't express my gratitude."

"Thank you," Bushkin replied.

Following that, Sonia and Bushkin excused themselves.

As they walked back to the apartment holding hands, Sonia said, "They're a nice couple. I've had a pleasant evening."

"We have a nice group of people here."

"I think it will be hard for you to leave this area."

"Now, yes. Look, let's let things develop between us. I want to work this out."

"I love you, Levi."

"I love you, Sonia."

The two entered the apartment and readied for bed.

The following morning Bushkin awoke first. Sonia awoke as Bushkin showered. When he came out of the shower, she saw a look in his eyes that she hadn't seen since he spoke on the Holocaust at the World Jewish Congress. His gaze was riveting. His manner intense. She knew not to speak to him, but to dress quietly for shul. It was the day of Yom Kippur.

They left together but hadn't yet spoken.

Meanwhile, Sasha was writing a note she intended to give to Levi following the service.

Dear Levi,

I'm going to end my relationship with Vasily.
I want, and need, to speak to you immediately.

Sasha

She put the note in her pocketbook and waited for Vasily Ginsberg. The chauffeur-driven limousine soon pulled up outside her apartment where she waited. She got in and sat by the door opposite from Vasily.

"I will drop you off," he told her. "I have to meet with my lawyers this morning. I will join you approximately forty-five minutes after the service begins."

"Make sure you make a grand entrance," said Sasha, "so everyone will notice you. Isn't that what you want?

"One day a year," she continued, "you can't be observant with everyone else? You're the worst."

Sasha entered the synagogue and sat in a row with Yakov and Sarah Potemkin, their children Joshua and Rachel; Isadore and Yetta Samonovich, Amos Sephard and Tatyana Samuelson.

"Sasha," said Yetta. "I'd like to introduce you to Sonia Norowitz. She is visiting from New York."

Norowitz, recognizing that Sasha was Levi's former significant other, greeted her with a cold, stiff handshake. She then excused herself and went to see Levi in his office.

"Who was that?" said Sasha quizzically.

"She's a friend of Levi's," said Yetta.

"What kind of friend do you mean?"

"Levi and she are going together."

"What?"

"Yes, they met in New York at the World Jewish Congress."

"Are they serious?"

"Yes."

Sasha slumped in her seat, distraught and visibly upset.

Amos Sephard tapped Yakov Potemkin on the shoulder and whispered, "How does Levi do it?"

"Do what?"

"Get women like that. I mean he throws Sasha out, who could win Miss Israel, and gets Sonia, who could be Hollywood's next sex goddess."

"It must be something with these literary types," replied Yakov. "Look, how did Arthur Miller get Marilyn Monroe?"

"I've got to start reading more," Sephard said. "To get those two I'd read <u>War and Peace</u>."

"I thought you were dyslexic," said Yakov.

"Then I'll read it in Hebrew."

The service was about to begin and Sonia returned to her row and sat next to Yetta Samonovich.

As she sat down, Bushkin appeared on the bemah. His soul was bare. He was in awe this day, Yom Kippur, the holiest of holy days.

He began to read:

"This is the Day of Awe."

"This is the day of decision."

"This is the day of our atonement. We confess our sins and repent this day."

"Throughout eternity, you are God, we have no other."

"Ba-re-chu et A-do-nai ha-me-vo-rach!"

"Praise the Lord, to whom our praise is due!"

"Ba-ruch A-do-nai ha-me-vo-rach le-o-lam va-ed!"

"Praise be the Lord, to whom our praise is due, now and for ever!"

"She-ma Yis-ra-eil: A-do-nai E-lo-hei-nu, A-do-nai E-chad!"

"Hear, O Israel: The Lord is our God, the Lord is One!"

"Ba-ruch sheim ke-vod mal-chu-to le-o-lam va-ed!"

"Blessed is His glorious kingdom for ever and ever!"

"May this day add meaning to our lives. Let contrition awaken our conscience, our common worship unite us in love, our memories of bondage impel us to help the oppressed."

Some forty-five minutes into the service, Vasily Ginsberg walked in. As he approached his seat next to Sasha, Bushkin stopped the service. Ginsberg sat down. Then Bushkin paused for an additional ten seconds as he stared at Ginsberg. He then said dryly, "I'd like to announce that services began at 10 a.m." A wave of snickering moved through the audience.

Sonia said to Yetta, "What's that all about?"

"Levi hates him. He goes with Sasha."

"Hate is a sinful emotion, something to be atoned for on this day," said Sonia.

"Then put Levi down," said Yetta, "as an unrepentant sinner. He hates him three hundred and sixty-five days a year."

As Ginsberg sat next to Sasha, Sonia observed, as he reached for Sasha's hand, she brushed it away.

Throughout the service, Sonia noticed how Sasha stared at Bushkin and the rapt and loving attention she paid his every move. She thought Sasha was one of the most remarkably beautiful women she had ever seen. She began to view her as an adversary.

Bushkin asked his congregants to offer a silent confession of repentance.

As he prepared for the Torah reading, Sonia, again, looked at Sasha and Vasily Ginsberg. He whispered something to her. She then looked at him contemptuously.

"What is with those two?" Sonia asked Yetta.

"It's a long story," she replied.

"Does it involve Levi?"

"Yes. Vasily and Sasha began seeing each other when she was living with Levi. Levi always detested him. I'll tell you his contempt for Vasily is such, he had to be physically restrained from going after him at a board of directors meeting."

"Levi?"

"We were all astonished. But I learned one thing about Levi, he has a fire inside of him."

As Bushkin finished the Haftarah portion, Yetta said to Sonia, "Let's listen to his sermon. You'll see what I mean."

Bushkin began his sermon, saying, "This is our holiest day. And yet this, our day of atonement, is no doubt, for most of us, a day of dilemma.

"We are asked to atone for our sins before God, and we come here to do so. Yet our dilemma is: Where is God? Is God dead?

"Eighteen months ago, when we were in hiding or awaiting execution in death camps, we thought God had abandoned us.

"Yet today we are here, before God, asking Him for atonement.

"Then where is God?

"Was He with us in the death camps?

"Did He help the Jews survive the roundup and slaughter?

"Our too-few numbers suggest otherwise.

"Then again, I ask: Where is God? My answer is: God is in our souls. For us to abandon God is to abandon our souls. For us to abandon our souls would be for us to act like our murderers, the infidels and religious hypocrites that they are.

"The religious hypocrites might evoke God's name in the form of Jesus Christ. Ironically, they recognize Christ, a Jew, as their Christian salvation and savior. Their version of Christianity might suggest that being a Jew is a crime, even though Christ was a rabbi. Hence, the Jew is to be destroyed, based on some twisted logic. Can these Christians who evoke Christ's name and then murder Jews truly have God in their soul?

"No. At that point, then, Christ is but an icon, a purely meaningless symbol. And a symbol to be exploited. The religious hypocrites might say that we commit this murder in the name of Christ, or we do horrible things in Christ's good name. But can these people claim to worship the Lord without having God in their soul?

"People who have God in their soul don't wantonly murder in the name of the Lord, nor do they do hurtful acts in his holy name. It is those who have kept God in their soul, that in view of what has happened to us, can repent in front of Him today. Because we have looked inside of us and have seen that God lives in our soul, we come here today, Yom Kippur, our holiest day and day of atonement. This--and only this--is why we can repent before him.

"Amen."

Bushkin then led the congregation in Kaddish, the prayer of mourning.

He said a prayer for Israel.

He announced that the next meeting of the board of directors would be in two weeks and that we would plan the celebration of the year anniversary since "we've moved into our synagogue and made it a permanent home."

He returned the Torah to the ark. As he stood before the congregation, he said, "Today we have repented before God. He lives in our souls where we are comfortable in giving Him a home and where He has dominion."

"Amen."

As the congregation contemplated his words, the majority of members moved slowly towards him. They formed a line, and he greeted each individually with hugs and handshakes.

When Sasha appeared before him, she had tears in her eyes. She hugged Bushkin passionately and, unbeknownst to him, slipped a note in his pocket. She whispered "I love you" in his ear and kissed him on the cheek.

Sonia, standing ten feet from Vasily Ginsberg, saw this and became visibly agitated. On the other hand, Ginsberg viewed this impassively and unemotionally.

After the line had dissipated, Sonia approached Bushkin. "Your words today were profound, emotional and exquisite. Now I know why I fell in love with you.

"You know," she continued, "she's very beautiful."

"Who?" replied Bushkin.

"Sasha."

"Come on, let's leave," he replied.

"You know your congregation loves you."

"I wouldn't say that."

"I think it will be hard for you to leave Ugograd."

"A smart man," replied Bushkin, "once told me the graveyard is full of indispensable people.

"Listen," he continued, "we are going to break fast tonight with Yakov and Sarah Potemkin. Let's go back to the apartment and change. It might be a nice afternoon to take a walk."

"Okay, rabbi," she said.

They held hands on the way back and said little. She wanted to talk about his previous relationship with Sasha, but couldn't find a logical segue. Sonia knew if she appeared to force the subject, he would become agitated and abrasive. She was also inquisitive about the contents of the note that Sasha had furtively slipped into his pocket.

"You're awfully quiet," said Bushkin. "Why?"

"I'm just thinking."

"About what?"

"Random thoughts," she answered.

They entered the apartment, changed and began to walk towards the campus.

"I'm enjoying myself tremendously," Sonia said.

"I'm glad you like it here. Tomorrow, while I have class, I want you to pick out some nice things at Sandler's."

"Isadore says he's going to give me a 'deal, deal.'"

"Pick out what you want. It's on me, but be sure to try it on for me."

"Sure."

"You know," Sonia said, "the High Holidays can be such a sad time when you think about all the friends and family that are deceased. Sometimes I feel guilty being a survivor. But being here is like being among extended family. I feel a certain joy being here with you and in this area."

"We're working hard to build a community. Ugograd was once a Jewish hub. We continue to attract survivors. Maybe one day, again, Ugograd will be a Jewish mecca.

"How about if we head back," said Bushkin.

As they walked back to the apartment, Sonia said, "It appears you're not too fond of Vasily Ginsberg."

"Please, Sonia, don't bring him up."

"Okay, I'm sorry. You don't have to get so angry."

"Please, don't bring him up," he repeated.

"The weather's nice," Sonia joked. "How about that for a change of pace?"

"Look, I'd rather walk in knee-deep snow than talk about Vasily Ginsberg."

"I see," she said. "You know I saw Sasha slip a letter to you. Would you mind sharing its contents with me?"

"You're prying and you're making me upset."

"I have a right to know what's in the letter."

"If I think you should know, I'll tell you."

"Are we going together or not?"

"Yes."

"Then what are you hiding?"

"What's addressed to me is my business."

"I saw how she whispered to you. I think she still loves you and you love her."

"You're making me upset. I'm going to call the Potemkins and tell them we're not coming."

"Don't be that way."

"Then stop prying and stop bringing up Vasily Ginsberg and Sasha."

"Okay, okay."

As they entered the apartment, Bushkin said, "I'm going to shower then get ready for dinner."

As he got into the shower, Sonia searched his pocket for the note. She saw he hadn't opened it, and knew, at that point, she had to put it back. Still, she remained absorbed by its suspected contents.

After Bushkin showered, Sonia bathed and the two dressed for dinner.

"Are you hungry?" Bushkin asked Sonia.

"Sure, aren't you?"

"Sundown will be soon. We will break the fast."

As they entered the Potemkin's, Yakov said, "I'm hungry, let's sit down and eat."

"It's not sundown," Bushkin replied. "Let's eat anyway," said Yakov. "By the way, how many members of the congregation do you think really fast?"

"I suspect," laughed Bushkin, as he sat down to dinner, "that most of them make it until breakfast."

"Did you see Hillel Hershkovitz?" said Sarah Potemkin. "He's as big as the Hindenburg. If he keeps eating, he won't be able to fit into his chair next year."

"I guess he fasts until dessert," quipped Sonia.

"Mommy," said Joshua Potemkin, "you didn't give me my allowance this week."

"You're not getting your allowance until you make your bed and empty your trash can."

"Then when I do that will you give me interest because the allowance is late?"

"Where does he get this from, Yakov?"

"Mommy," said Joshua, "when I get older and join daddy's law firm, I'm going to sue you because you didn't pay me my allowance."

"You do that and you'll be coming to court with a red tushy."

"I can see it now," said Sarah, "Rachel Potemkin, our daughter, will make her concert debut. She will play the Tchaikovsky Piano Concerto Number One. Her technique, her interpretation, her emotion will mesmerize the audience and astound the critics. And in the middle of the second movement, a crew will come on stage and start rolling the piano off. And the auctioneer will announce, 'By order of Joshua Potemkin, the mortgage holder, the building is being auctioned off because the mortgage is unpaid.'

"When they ask Joshua why he wouldn't let his sister finish, he'll say, 'I would have lost ten minutes worth of interest.'

"You see, Sonia, my side of the family had culture. We played the piano, we discussed French literature, we talked about philosophy and we read poetry."

"Sarah," said Yakov, "the next time you go to the store and buy a dress, I'll give you a poem by Robert Browning. See if the store accepts it as a payment and let me know how much change the cashier gives you. If the store takes a poem, I'll give up law, become an intellectual and write poetry."

"Don't listen to him, Sonia. His side had all the ganofs. Take his Uncle Max, ahavas shalom. We were newly married and Uncle Max was going to rent us an apartment. He told me he was giving it to us for $10 dollars a month under market. I thanked and hugged him. Then he showed us the apartment. I wouldn't keep a dog in there. I said, 'Uncle Max, aren't you going to paint?' He said, 'Yeah, we supply the paint job.' So he walked out into the hall and brought back two buckets of white paint and two brushes. And he told us in his properties 'the tenants paint.' He saw how agitated I was; so he said don't be upset, after you paint, you can keep the brushes. Then he said when it's finished it will be beautiful. I said, 'Uncle Max, is your idea of a beautiful apartment one where the ceiling hasn't fallen in in the last three weeks?'

"And when you were around him all he did was complain. The tenants were screwing him he said by wrecking his 'gorgeous' apartments; the housing inspectors were screwing him because of the way they enforced the code; and the banks were screwing him by charging him too much interest. At times I think the only person not screwing Uncle Max was his wife, which I could understand."

"If you think my side of the family was crazy," said Yakov, "wait till you hear this. On her side they were all impractical intellectuals. They 'intellectualized' over everything. That was the only family that could spend forty-five minutes intellectualizing over a bar of soap."

"And when my family had their deep discussions," said Sarah, "Yakov would walk out, just leave without saying excuse me. He was so rude."

"Rude. How many times did I have to hear that Descartes influenced Baruch Spinoza?

"Your family, if one of them would have managed a fast-food restaurant or had to meet a payroll, he would have had a nervous breakdown."

"Gee," said Sonia dryly, "and I thought all the crazy Jews lived in New York."

206

"We've been working to change that for months," laughed Yakov.

"Sonia," said Joshua, "if you're not going to finish your food, can I eat yours?"

"Sure, handsome."

"Yakov, I want you to talk to him; he's eating too much and I'm worried he's going to get too heavy."

"I'll talk to him. I'll talk to him."

"Sonia," said Joshua, "the next time you're in town, call me. We'll do lunch. I've got some big plans that I want to discuss with you."

"Sure," said Sarah, "big plans. I'll be the only mother afraid to use her son's law firm. I'll be late paying a bill, and he'll have me in the office scrubbing the floors to work it off."

"Mommy," said Rachel Potemkin, "may I be excused to play the piano?"

"Yes, angel face. Why don't we have coffee and dessert in the living room and listen to Rachel play the piano?"

"What should I play, Mommy?"

"Play Brahms' Lullaby, doll face."

"You'll make a mistake. You'll make a mistake," sang Joshua.

"Is that nice, Joshua? Apologize to your sister."

Rachel sat down and played the piece.

"Bravo, Bravo," said Bushkin as she finished. "Well done," echoed Sonia.

"Children, please go upstairs and do your homework. Remember, Joshua, no allowance until you take out your trash and make your bed."

"Yakov, I want you to talk to him about his big mouth."

"I'll talk to him. I'll talk to him."

"Look, it's been a long day. Yakov and Sarah, if you don't mind, Sonia and I would like to excuse ourselves and spend some time together. She'll be leaving soon."

"I understand," said Yakov.

As the couples were about to exchange their good-byes at the door, Joshua yelled downstairs from the top step, "Mommy, can I say good-bye to Sonia?"

"Yes."

Joshua came down from the top step and said, "Can I give you a kiss, Sonia, until we meet again?"

"Sure."

"Yakov, tell that nine-year-old Cassanova that he'll get no allowance until he makes his bed."

"I'll talk to him. I'll talk to him."

The couples then exchanged good-byes.

As they walked back to the apartment, Bushkin said, "Remember, Sonia, I want you to go to Sandler's tomorrow and pick out some nice dresses. Then bring them over to the office and try them on for me."

"Sure."

The next morning the couple awoke early.

"You know, Sonia," Bushkin said as he held her tightly, "I told the congregation six months ago that it should begin looking for another rabbi.

"I could move to New York and we could be married. I could always get a teaching job there and I'd have time to write. I'd love to do a memoir based on my recent experience and then a novel."

"I hope I'm part of your memoir, darling."

"You will be, Sonia. You will be."

"How?"

"It's all going to work out. It's all going to work out," he said as he began to kiss her lovingly about the face and neck.

Bushkin soon left for work. Early in the afternoon, Sonia came into the office and tried on one of the dresses. It was a form-fitting black dress with a low neck and back line. She modeled it for him, turning around slowly.

"My God," said Bushkin, "when they made you, they didn't neglect too many details."

The following morning, Sonia packed to leave. Bushkin, because he had a late class, accompanied her to the airport. As he waited for her to board the plane, he said, "I'll see you here on Thanksgiving. Then I'll come to New York between Christmas and New Year's. I want this to happen."

As she got ready to board, she hugged him and said, "You know she's very beautiful."

"To whom are you referring?"

"Sasha."

# Chapter XXI

## Sasha, Again

He returned to the apartment after Sonia boarded her plane and flew back to New York. He took Sasha's note out and read it for the first time.

At first Bushkin was indifferent to the message that she was going to end her relationship with Vasily Ginsberg and she wanted to speak to him immediately. He left the note on top of the desk. He exited the room where the note was but soon returned to reread it. Bushkin knew he still had feelings for her and began to call Sasha, but hung up the phone before the call could be completed. He decided it would be best if he could suppress his feelings for her.

Bushkin then walked to the University to teach his afternoon class. He returned home that evening to prepare the agenda for the upcoming board of directors meeting, which was still nearly two weeks away. After he had earlier reread the note, Bushkin knew Sasha would attend her first meeting in some seven months.

The night of the meeting, Sasha, as expected, appeared. Except for Vasily Ginsberg, all other directors were present: Bushkin, Yakov and Sarah Potemkin, Isadore and Yetta Samonovich, Amos Sephard and Tatyana Samuelson.

With the assembled present, Bushkin began the meeting a few minutes early. As he did, Isadore Samonovich said to Bushkin, "Why don't you wait until the scheduled time to begin, as Vasily Ginsberg might appear?"

Bushkin looked at him disdainfully, and brought up the first order of business.

"Mr. Ginsberg's promised contribution is way past due. Yakov, please contact him again to see when, and if, we can expect the money. Again, Yakov," said Bushkin, as he cast a melting stare in the direction of Sasha, "I have a standing bet with you, if you want to take me up on it, that we'll never see his promised contribution."

With his cold stare still riveted on Sasha, he said, "By the way, Yakov, did you get a chance to view Mr. Ginsberg's prospectus for his public offering?"

"Yes," he replied.

"Well, what are your thoughts?"

"It's tantamount to fraud, but I believe he'll be able to sell the shares."

"Great," said Bushkin, his cold eyes still trained on Sasha. "I can read the headlines now, 'Jew Financier Defrauds Countrymen,' and 'Ginsberg Indicted Again for Securities Fraud.' That's all we need."

"By the time the trial occurs," said Yakov, "you might be married and living in New York."

Ignoring that response, Bushkin turned towards Yakov and said, "Who would defend that son-of-a-bitch?"

"Don't be naive," he replied. "Every lawyer in the country would defend him. Look, for money, we'd all go to court and swear a dog is a cat."

"Aren't you in a wonderful profession, Yakov?"

"It's no worse than most of the others," he replied.

"As you know," Bushkin continued, now again staring at Sasha, "I've met someone and I may be getting married next year and moving to New York. It's time for a committee to be formed to look for a new rabbi.

"Volunteers, please."

When no one volunteered, he said, "Sasha, why don't you serve with Amos and Isadore?"

"I'm not interested," she said. "How about you, Yetta?"

"Okay."

"Please return next month with a progress report," he told the committee.

"As you are aware," said Bushkin, "we will soon celebrate our one-year anniversary since we moved into our synagogue.

"What I'm thinking is that we have a Shabbos dinner and, following the service, an Oneg Shabbat.

"Who will help me plan the dinner?"

"I will," said Sasha.

Ignoring Sasha, Bushkin said, "How about Tatyana and Sarah assisting me?"

"Okay," said Sarah.

"I'd prefer if Sasha served instead of me," said Tatyana. "I'm extremely busy."

"It won't take long, Tatyana."

"Okay, you win," she replied.

"Since we are pressed for time, I would prefer if the committee to plan the anniversary celebration meets here tomorrow night."

Both Tatyana and Sarah agreed to do so.

The following day in her apartment studio, Tatyana received a call from Sasha.

"I spoke to Levi," she said, "and if it's okay with you, I will take your place on the committee."

"Thank you. Thank you. Thank you," Tatyana said. "I'm just too busy to do any more. That was very thoughtful of you to take my place."

"Not really," replied Sasha as she hung up.

The following night, as Sarah and Levi were waiting for Tatyana to come in to begin the meeting, they were surprised to see Sasha enter the room.

"Tatyana said she was busy and asked me to take her place," said Sasha.

"I don't think so, doctor," replied Bushkin.

"Get off your high horse, rabbi," yelled Sasha.

"Stop it, you two," said Sarah, "or I'm leaving. We can't have a meeting with you bickering at one another."

Bushkin then began the committee meeting. "On the first Friday night in November," he said, "the celebration will take place. Why don't we have a Sabbath dinner of chicken or brisket, a vegetable and a potato? We should expect one hundred people and, to be safe, we will order sixty dishes of each. We can give what isn't eaten to the Ugograd Orphanage."

"Sounds reasonable," says Sasha.

"Okay, Sasha, please take care of ordering the food."

"Yes, rabbi."

"Sarah," said Bushkin, "could you make sure the notices are sent out?"

"I'll do that too," volunteered Sasha.

"Sarah, could you please talk to Irena Goldsmith, our violinist with the Ugograd Symphony, about contracting for music?"

"Sure."

"I think," continued Bushkin, "if we have two violins, a cello and a piano, that ensemble might be appropriate. However, talk to Irena about what's best."

"Should I ask Irena to play?"

"No," quipped Bushkin, "let's give her a night off."

"I'll take care of ordering the desserts for dinner and the Oneg Shabbat.

"Sasha, when you order the food, don't accept the caterer's first price. We are ordering in bulk. We're entitled to a discount."

"Understood," she said.

"By the way," he said staring at Sasha, "if Vasily Ginsberg would have given us the promised contribution, we could have afforded a more elaborate celebration."

"Why are you so obsessed with Vasily?" said Sarah indignantly.

"Why don't you ask Sasha?" he shot back.

"Why don't you shut up," said Sasha. "You're acting like a petulant two-year-old."

"Is that so," said Bushkin.

"Look," said Sarah, "one more outburst, and you can get someone else to take my place."

"Well, it's her fault. Tatyana was supposed to serve on this committee."

"That's it, I'm leaving."

"I'm sorry, Sarah," he said as he took her hand. "It's my fault."

"Apologize to Sasha and then step outside for a minute or two to relieve your anger."

"I apologize, Sasha."

When he left the room, Sarah asked, "Why does he act that way?"

"He always despised Vasily and now he's mad at me."

"You know what I think, Sasha?"

"What?"

"I think he cares for you very deeply--more so than you can imagine. Sometimes emotions get twisted and love turns to hate, temporarily. If he didn't care about you, he wouldn't act this way. If he didn't feel for you, he would be far more dispassionate and would be oblivious to your presence. I think he still loves you, deeply."

When Bushkin returned, he asked if there was any more business to discuss.

"No," said Sasha and Sarah.

"If we have questions or need clarifications, we can contact each other by phone. If necessary," said Bushkin, "we can meet again. Let's adjourn for the evening and I'll lock up."

Following the adjournment, Sarah left immediately.

"Levi."

"What is it, Sasha?"

"Can you walk me back to my apartment?"

"I'd rather not."

"Did you read my note?"

"Yes."

"I'd like to see if we can begin again. I love you, even though you were acting childish tonight."

"I didn't start seeing Vasily."

"I made a mistake. You were right."

"You understand, of course, that I'm going with someone."

"I do and she's very attractive."

"Thank you, and she's very special to me, too."

"Please walk me back to my apartment."

"Okay. You know, Sasha, you're looking exceptionally beautiful tonight."

"Thank you."

"How are things at the hospital?"

"Busy, anxious and hectic."

"I can imagine."

"I miss you, Levi. Hold my hand."

"Okay. Isn't this where you live?"

"How did you know?"

"I went through the membership roster."

"Why?"

"Because I was inquisitive to see where you lived."

"Why?"

"Because at one time I loved you and wanted to marry you."

Now at the front door, Sasha put her arms around Levi and pressed her body against his. He put his arms around her and their faces touched. They closed their eyes. He began to rub his hands passionately all over her back.

She then pushed him away.

"Good night, rabbi," she said.

He thought about following her in but decided against it.

The next morning he got a call at his office. It was Sasha.

"Levi," she said quickly, "I made arrangements with the caterer. I negotiated hard and got twenty percent off. I didn't want to push him beyond that point. He was really getting irritated."

"Make sure, Sasha, that he understands with the discount we still expect the same level of service."

"I will, darling."

A few minutes later the phone rang.

"Levi, darling, the caterer understands everything. Is there any more I can do?"

"Remember to get out the notices."

"Of course, darling.

"Levi, why don't you and I have lunch one day soon?"

"What for?"

"To discuss the celebration?"

"I don't think that will be necessary."

"I do."

"Okay, a week from today, noon. I'll meet you at your office."

"Good-bye, darling," she said as she hung up.

"Nadia," Sasha said to Nadia Pavel, her assistant, "have some coffee with me."

"You seem very happy this morning, Sasha."

"Well, I was with Levi last night."

"I'm sure you will tell me all about it."

"I will," she said as they sat in a corner booth in the hospital cafeteria.

"I think I can get back with him, but there is still anger on his part towards me.

"He knows I'm breaking up with Vasily Ginsberg, but the difficult problem is that he has met someone and they're serious. She lives in New York and she is extremely attractive."

"What gives you cause for optimism?"

"We were together last night, and after some problems, he walked me back to my apartment. We then held each other affectionately and our faces touched. I know he felt what I felt. I then pushed him away, hoping he'd follow me inside.

"Though he didn't, we spoke again this morning and have a luncheon date next week.

"He knows where I live, and I asked him how he knew. He said 'because once I loved you and wanted to marry you.' Previous to that, I told him I loved him and wanted to 'begin again.'"

"What makes him so special?"

"He's kind, decent and honest. I should have never started seeing Vasily, but the temptation was too great. I judged a book by its cover, and I was wrong."

"How badly do you miss him?"

"Terribly."

"Why?"

"To tell you the truth, I miss everything about him. I even miss our arguments, and when we had them, they were beauties. What I could never understand is that when we argued, neither of us was wrong, yet we couldn't agree on anything. So he'd scream at me, and I'd scream at him. Then we made up and that was beautiful.

"Or, if I had a hard day, he'd take me in his arms and start reciting extemporaneous poetry.

"He'd say things to reassure me like:

'To hold and behold you is my reason for being.

'Being without you I'm doubtful that I'm worth being.

'With you I soar, without you I'm not sure.

'Stay with me, stay with me and make my life worth being.'"

"My God, he'd tell you things like that, Sasha?"

"All the time."

"Sasha, if you don't grab this guy up, I will."

"I'm trying. I'm trying. Besides, he'd never date someone outside his religion."

"I'll convert."

"Be serious."

"I am."

"Nadia," said Sasha irately, "it's getting late, let's get back to work."

Bushkin received a call from Olga Tereshnova of the Informant. "The Ugograd Hebrew Congregation will soon have its one-year anniversary since it moved to its synagogue. Do you plan a celebration?"

"Ms. Tereshnova, before I answer, I want to make it perfectly clear that I want the story reported straight. I don't want your piece to inflame the anti-Semitic elements in the country. I have a responsibility to our membership."

"Haven't you been helped by the Informant's publicity?"

"Yes, but I'm always concerned about the tone and context of the articles. I want this story to be positive, not inflammatory."

"Some people," replied Tereshnova, "are inflamed by the mention of the word 'Jew.'"

"I don't want you to be the one inflaming them."

"Can we begin the interview, Dr. Bushkin?"

"Yes."

"It will soon be a year since your congregation has moved into its synagogue. What are thoughts at this time?"

"We are happy to be living in comparative peace and as Jews. This is important to us, and we are heartened as more Jewish survivors have made Ugograd their home. Our synagogue, our permanent home, then, stands as a symbol of hope and a beacon to our future."

"What activities do you plan on the anniversary?"

"We will have a Sabbath dinner, a service, then a dessert. We will have music at the dinner. I think, though, these activities are far less significant than the event, that follows a Holocaust, where our numbers have been decimated almost to the point of extinction. The fact that our relatively small numbers, here and abroad, remain united is the far larger story. Our congregation, as far as I'm concerned, is but a link in the chain."

"Do you worry about an anti-Semitic outburst in the wake of the celebration?"

"I'm not going to comment on that. If I see one reference, no matter how subtle, to a possible anti-Semitic outburst in the article, I'm going to cancel the celebration and tell your editor you've abused my trust."

"I understand. Who is working on the celebration?"

"It is a committee composed of me, Sarah Potemkin and Dr. Sasha Liebowitz."

"Aren't you and Dr. Liebowitz living together?"

"We've broken up."

"Dr. Bushkin, I understand you are still acting rabbi."

"Yes, but a committee has been empowered to search for a permanent replacement."

"Do you have anything you want to add?"

"No."

"Thank you for your time."

"Thank you and good-bye."

"Tereshnova then called Andrei Traicov of the anti-Semitic National Organization (NO). "Do you know the Ugograd Hebrew Congregation will celebrate its one-year anniversary since it moved into its synagogue?"

"Tell me more."

"The congregation will have a dinner, service and dessert on the Jewish Sabbath on the first Friday night in November. Do you wish to comment?"

Traicov hung up.

The day of his lunch with Sasha, Bushkin thought about calling her to cancel, but then decided against it. He met Sasha in her office at noon.

"You look lovely, today," he told her. "Where do you want to go?"

"How about the hospital cafeteria?"

"Fine."

They sat down.

"You know I meant what I said when I told you I love you," said Sasha.

"Thomas Wolfe, the novelist, wrote <u>You Can't Go Home Again</u>. There's a lot of truth to that."

"I remember that you explained to me the meaning of the Renaissance, the revival of literature and art, with its great humanistic expansion. You discussed with me Petrarch, Boccaccio, Leonardo and Michelangelo. You talked to me about humanists overcoming self-imposed dogma and constraints. You taught me to think in terms of possibilities, which I am as I look at you."

"Sasha, you look so beautiful--inside and out."

"You know what I remember, Levi?"

221

"What?"

"When we met, and how you were so attracted to me and I to you. And how we teased each other. And how I insisted on getting a two-bedroom apartment. And how you escalated the teasing and got a two-bedroom and a den, insisting that the den be large enough to be converted into a third bedroom. Then you locked me out. When I pounded on the door, you asked me, 'Is that you, doctor?' always emphasizing the 'd' as if to put me, once and for all, in my place. But I loved when you did that. I remember when we made love that night. It was such a beautiful experience. No matter what happens between us, Levi, I will never forget you. I loved you then and I love you now. You're the one who is beautiful inside and out."

"Sasha, if we don't order soon, I'm going to cry."

"Levi, if you start crying, I'll start crying."

The two started staring at each other, lovingly. A waitress came over but decided not to interrupt and walked away. The couple didn't notice her.

"I can't eat now, Sasha. Let's take a walk. Maybe we'll eat some fruit and drink a soda along the way."

"Okay."

As the two walked, the day was cool and crisp with a bit of a chill in the air, and there was a strong breeze that tousled Sasha's hair.

"When the wind blows your hair like that, Sasha, it accentuates your beauty. You're so lovely."

"Levi, let's stop here at this fruit stand. How about if we get some apples and sodas?"

"Fine."

"Let's share this apple, Levi."

"Sure."

As they passed the apple back and forth, each taking a bite, they gloried and took comfort in each other's company.

"You know, Levi, when I'm with you now, it seems we've never been apart. It feels wonderful."

"Maybe your analogy," he said, "to the Renaissance is applicable after all. Yes, the Renaissance was very powerful."

"More powerful than Thomas Wolfe?"

"I would say so."

He put his arm around her shoulder as they walked back to her office. As they walked, he took a bite of the second apple and then fed it to her. The two each took alternative bites until it was finished. Then they drank from the same can of soda. As they came back to Sasha's office, they embraced tenderly and kissed.

Sasha entered the office.

Nadia said, "Sasha, you look happy."

"I feel happy," she replied.

# Chapter XXII

## No to the Jews, Yes to Sasha

"Sarah," said Bushkin during the phone call, "I'm assuming you've arranged the final details."

"Yes. Irena Goldsmith said a quartet of two violins, cello and a piano is appropriate. She gave me the names of the musicians and I've phoned them. However, Irena wants to play an opening solo."

"What does she wish to play?"

"Hatikvah."

"She's a survivor; so she'll play it with her soul."

"I know she will," said Sarah.

Bushkin next called Sasha. "Did you make all the arrangements?"

"Yes, darling. The food has been ordered, and the notices were mailed yesterday.

"Look, Levi," she continued, "on the night of our celebration, I'm going to tell Vasily that I no longer wish to see him. It's over between us, regardless of what might eventually happen between you and me."

"I understand."

"Is that all you can say?"

"What should I say?"

"Say what you feel."

"You're doing the right thing, regardless of what may happen between us."

"You can't say anything beyond that?"

"Right now, no."

"Good-bye, Levi."

"Good-bye, Sasha."

Reacting and speaking quickly, Sasha said, "Before you hang up, Levi, I want to tell you one thing."

"What's that?"

"I love you."

"Good-bye, Sasha," he said as he hung up the phone.

At the meeting of the National Organization (NO), Andrei Traicov addressed the membership. "The Ugograd Hebrew Congregation will celebrate its one-year anniversary since it moved to its synagogue."

A voice yells out from the crowd, "Let's give the Jew-bastards a celebration they'll never forget."

"My thoughts exactly," said Traicov. The audience erupted with wild cheering and blood-curdling yells.

"We will be armed that night. We can lure the Jew-bastards outside and murder them. Then, when that's done, we'll burn down the synagogue. Who's with me?"

"We all are," yelled another voice from the audience.

"Alexander."

"What is it Yevgeny?"

"Didn't that lady Jew-doctor save your life?"

"So, she's a Jew, isn't she?"

"You're right, Alexander."

Father Yosef Vagins put down his edition of the Informant and immediately called Bushkin. "Levi, are you free today to meet?"

"Certainly, Father."

"Three p.m. at my office, Levi."

"I'll be there," he said.

Bushkin arrived precisely at 3 p.m. and sat in a comfortable leather chair in front of Vagins.

"How is my Jewish friend?" Vagins asked.

"Fine, Father. What is the purpose of this meeting?"

"Levi, I've read where the Ugograd Hebrew Congregation will celebrate the year anniversary since it moved to its synagogue."

"That's right."

"Are you going to have adequate security the night of the celebration?"

"Frankly, I've given it some thought, but haven't contracted for any yet."

"Don't be naive, Levi. That ought to be your first priority. I think NO will make a move that evening. Expect the worst."

"You're right, Father."

When Bushkin returned to his office, he contracted with City Security for two armed guards.

Later that day the president of City Security, Titan Klukev, phoned Traicov. "Bushkin, the Jew, phoned us for security the night of the celebration."

"I'm sure," said Traicov, "you will give him 'security' that he'll never forget."

Klukev, laughing, hung up.

The night of the event, the congregants gathered at 6:15 p.m. for dinner. Irena Goldsmith began the program with Hatikvah. Her presentation, expression and tone enraptured the audience. Those present were transfixed by her passion and the character of her play as the gripping melody began to dance off her strings. The membership began to hum along with her.

Hatikvah, the Israeli national anthem, was their anthem, their melody, and the song of their Jewishness.

When she finished at first the audience was silent, then it applauded respectfully. The gathering had been touched deeply. Bushkin said thank you. She nodded in his direction. He began to applaud again; then the members joined him in his applause which lasted for nearly a minute and defined their appreciation.

She bowed to the congregants. Many, in turn, bowed to her and she sat down.

Dinner was being served. Joshua Potemkin said the Bracha over the bread: "Bo-ruch a-toh A-do-noy, E-loo-hay-noo me-lech ho-o-lom, ha-mo-tzee le-chem meen ho-o-retz."

"Blessed art Thou, O Lord, our God, King of the Universe, Who bringest forth bread from the earth."

He then said the Bracha over the wine.

"Bo-ruch a-toh A-do-noy E-lo-hay-noo me-lech ho-l-om, bo-ray p'ree ha-go-fen."

"Blessed art Thou, O Lord our God, King of the Universe, Who createst the fruit of the vine."

"Good job, boychik," said Amos Sephard, who was seated at the head table with the directors: Levi Bushkin, Tatyana Samuelson, Sasha Liebowitz, Vasily Ginsberg, Sasha's escort; Isadore and Yetta Samonovich and Yakov and Sarah Potemkin, along with their children, Rachel and Joshua.

"Yakov," said Bushkin, "please ask Vasily Ginsberg when we can expect his contribution. In the meantime, I'm going outside to make sure our security is in place. Please excuse me."

A few minutes later he returned.

"Yakov, did you ask Mr. Ginsberg about his contribution?"

"Yes."

"What did he say?"

"Next week, for sure."

"Next week of what year?" replied Bushkin sarcastically.

"Joshua."

"What is it, Mommy?"

"You're eating too fast. No one is going to take it away from you."

"I'm hungry."

"Are you ever not hungry?"

"Leave him alone, Sarah," said Amos Sephard. "He's a growing boy."

"Amos, if he keeps growing like this, I'm afraid he's going to grow sideways."

"He's a good boy, Sarah."

"When he sleeps!" she replied.

"My God, Joshua," said Sarah, "you're already finished, and I haven't even started."

"Mommy, where is the extra food?"

"Over in the corner."

"May I be excused to get seconds?"

"Yes, Joshua. But you're eating too much and too fast."

Following dinner, the congregation entered the area of worship and began the service.

During the sermon, Bushkin said, "Tonight we are here to celebrate the year anniversary since we've moved to our synagogue.

"This has not been an easy year for any of us. Because of the Holocaust, we continue to mourn the loss of family and friends. And, as survivors, we continue to feel guilty because so many of our co-religionists have died. We have asked ourselves why do we live when so many have died.

"Many of us have been uprooted and have come to Ugograd, a strange city, to look for opportunity and be among our fellow Jews.

"So we are here, in spite of our numbers being thinned to levels of near extinction, living and worshipping as Jews.

"And yet we are here, too, as mishpachah, even though our nuclear families have either been partly or completely destroyed. So look at the person next to you. Take his or her hand and hold it. This is our family. As our hands touch, we have formed a family tree.

"Let's remember this always. We have risen above the Holocaust. We are survivors. We not only have a kinship with one another, but with our brethren who survive the world over.

"Amen."

"We will conclude this service with the watchword of our faith as we recite Shema in unison."

As Bushkin and the congregation began the Shema, he began to hear noise from outside the building and then what seemed like a muffled roar. Then he heard screaming. Someone yelled, "Kill the Jews." He came down from the bemah, walked down the aisle and out the front door. He was astonished to see a mob of approximately one hundred and fifty people bearing torches and rifles. Some held signs proclaiming "Hitler Was Right" and "Let This Solution Be The Final Solution."

Sasha and some of the other congregants followed him outside. In front of the mob was Andrei Traicov and Alexander Shukov, whose body Sasha had surgically repaired and whose life she saved. Fatalistically, Sasha always knew this day would come. In an instant she remembered lines from a letter she wrote Mary Shukov: "How ironic and sad the religious murderer, the Jew killer, lives, and the civilized, because of their religion, died. And how ironic is it that he may yet murder me, his Jewish savior."

As Traicov, Shukov and their cadre advanced, Bushkin met them on the top step. Jamming his index finger in Traicov's chest, Bushkin told him, "You will not take another step forward."

As Traicov moved to slap Bushkin's hand away, Bushkin saw something rush at him from the corner of his eye, but couldn't react quickly enough to avoid the contact. He was hit hard from the side and rolled over twice. When he looked up, he was astonished to see Father Vagins dressed in a dark suit with a large silver cross that hung around his neck.

In front of the mob, Vagins raised his hands.

"You will advance no further," he told them.

"Kill the Jew-lover," yelled a voice from the mob.

Vagins then dropped his arms and trained his index finger over the width of the crowd.

"Who among you has access to wooden posts?" he said in a voice that was deep, throaty and intense.

"I do, Jew-lover."

"Then bring them," said Vagins angrily.

"Who also among you has access to rope and nails?" said an enraged Vagins.

"I do," said another voice from the mob.

"Then you bring them, too," said Vagins in a voice that continued to raise in intensity and emotion.

"Before you touch any of my Jewish brothers," Vagins screamed angrily at the crowd, "you will crucify me first on these synagogue steps. Then let the world see what you've done."

The mob stopped in stunned amazement. The silence became deafening. The Jews behind Vagins on the landing looked on with equal astonishment. The only sound that could be heard was that of Joshua Potemkin biting into an apple as he leaned against a synagogue wall.

Finally, the mob in front of Vagins began to mill around. Then it began to disperse, slowly. The confrontation had been defused.

Vagins and Sasha came over to Bushkin, who was still lying on the ground. "Are you okay?" they asked.

"Sure," he replied.

"Maybe you'd better stay down for a moment, you took a hard fall," said Sasha.

"I'm okay, Sasha."

"Levi, I'm going to go," said Vagins.

"You saved us, Father."

"No, I saved humanity."

As Vagins walked down the synagogue steps, Amos Sephard and Yakov Potemkin came over to Bushkin, who was still lying on the ground.

"Are you okay?" Yakov asked.

"Yes, Yakov. I wish everyone would stop asking me how I am."

"Why don't you get up?"

"Sasha thinks I should lie here for a while to make sure I'm all right. She's the doctor."

"Yakov," said Amos, "it's a good thing Father Vagins thinks he's Jesus Christ."

"It's a good thing that maybe he is," replied Yakov.

Before Bushkin could get up, Vasily Ginsberg came over to where Sasha was attending him.

"What a performance everyone put on," he said cynically. "Anyone with sense knew nothing was going to happen."

"How can you say that, you unadulterated louse?" said Sasha.

"Come on, Sasha, let's go," he told her.

"I'm staying with Levi," she replied. "He needs me."

Ginsberg, reaching for her arm, tried to pull her away. She pushed his hand away. Again he tried and again she pushed his hand away.

"Leave her alone, Vasily," Bushkin told him.

Ginsberg walked away in disgust.

"May I get up now, Sasha?

"Are you sure you're all right?"

"Sasha, I'm all right."

"Don't get up too quickly."

Bushkin, getting up slowly, said, "Sasha, come into the synagogue with me. I want to report this incident to the police. Then I will lock up." After he dialed the police, he was kept on hold for five minutes without anyone responding.

"I'll call the police in the morning and make a report," he said. "I'll lock up and then we will go." After he turned off the lights and locked up, he said to Sasha, "Let's leave."

"Aren't you going to call a cab," she said, "to take us back?"

"We're going to walk."

"Are you crazy? Are you suicidal, Levi?"

"I want them to see us walk back. They are just as afraid of us as we are of them."

"Aren't you scared, Levi?"

"I hope I don't urinate in my pants on the way."

"We're crazy to do this, Levi."

"Walk at a regular pace, Sasha, and act normally."

"Okay. Levi, you were very brave to stand up to that mob."

"That wasn't bravery. That was rage. If I had had my wits about me, I would have run. We all would have run. I'm no hero."

"To me, you're a hero."

"That was sweet of you, Sasha. If there was a hero tonight, it was Father Vagins. He put his life on the line for us. He's a beautiful, selfless human being. He's what Christianity and Christ's teachings are about. He's a true Christian and a great man."

At that moment a car drove by, and through an open window a passenger yelled "Jew" at Bushkin and Sasha as they continued to walk.

"Levi, I'm scared."

"I'm petrified, too, but keep walking normally. They're bullies. When you stand up to them, they won't know how to react except as the cowards they really are."

"Levi, why are you turning here?"

"I'm walking you back to your apartment."

"Levi, please let me stay with you tonight--just tonight. I'm scared. Besides, you may have a reaction from your fall. You may need medical help."

"Sasha, since when did you become such an 'angel of mercy?'"

"Since I met you."

"Okay, we'll go back to my apartment, but I won't sleep with you."

"Did I ask you to?"

"Okay, so long as we understand one another."

"We do, Levi. What can I wear to bed?"

"Wear one of my robes."

As the couple entered the apartment, Bushkin said, "Sasha, I'm going to bed. I'm all keyed up, but I'm going to try to fall asleep."

As Bushkin turned in, he locked his bedroom door, and, though restless, was able to eventually fall asleep.

"Levi, Levi," Sasha screamed, pounding on his bedroom door. "I smell something. It might be gas. Maybe we're being attacked."

Bushkin rushed to the door and opened it. There stood Sasha in front of him in Bushkin's robe, which was open in the front. She grabbed his pajama top and tried to wrestle him to his bed. He permitted her to do so. The two fell into bed. Their passion was frantic. Sasha's aggressiveness, as it had in the past, titillated him. She knew no inhibitions, nor did she want to. She locked her body to his in a loving sexual union. She knew she wanted Bushkin more than anything, and she wanted her sexuality to demonstrate this. As the two consummated their love making, Bushkin looked lovingly at her and stroked the hair on her forehead.

"You little jerk," he said to her.

"You big idiot," she replied.

With those words, they began another frantic session of love making. After they consummated this session, Bushkin said, "You're sure making things complicated."

"Levi," she replied, "you said you wouldn't sleep with me, so goodnight."

As she got out of bed and began to walk towards the door, Bushkin leaned over the edge of the bed and yanked her by the arm.

She fell into the bed, backwards.

"When I said I wouldn't sleep with you, I didn't say what night, doctor."

"Now I see," she said, laughing.

The two eventually fell asleep in each other's arms.

The next morning, when they awoke, Bushkin asked her, "Will you marry me?"

"Are you serious?" she replied.

"Of course," he said as he reached into a drawer and pulled out a diamond ring.

"Put it on," he told her.

"It fits fine," she said.

"Do you want to marry me?"

"Yes."

"Okay, we're now engaged and we'll soon set a wedding date."

"What should I do with my apartment, Levi?"

"Give it to Joshua Potemkin. Maybe he'll eat it."

# Chapter XXIII

## New Beginnings

"Sasha, I heard about what happened at the synagogue Friday night," said Nadia Pavel, her assistant. "I tried to call you over the weekend but you weren't in. Are you all right?"

"I'm fine."

"I see the ring on your finger. Are you engaged?"

"Yes."

"To whom?"

"Whom do you think?"

"I hope it's Levi."

"It is."

"Congratulations. How did it happen?"

"Well, Friday night we were almost murdered by an anti-Semitic mob, one of whom was Alexander Shukov, whom I had saved in surgery. Following the confrontation, during which we were saved by Father Vagins, Levi and I walked back to his apartment. He told me he wouldn't sleep with me. After he fell asleep I began pounding on his door, telling him I smelled something that might be gas and we might be under attack. When he opened the door I grabbed him. We fell into bed and made love.

"When we woke up Saturday, he asked me to marry him. I asked him if he was 'serious.'

"He said 'Yes.'

"We're now engaged and we will soon set a wedding date."

"Oh," replied Nadia, "so you had an uneventful weekend."

"Yes," said Sasha, "dull, boring and without incident. I hope you can suggest something to spice up my life," she added dryly.

"Maybe you can take dancing lessons."

"Interesting and worth exploring," said Sasha. "That might be just what I need."

That Monday morning Levi wrote to Sonia:

Dear Sonia,

This is extremely difficult for me to tell you, but I've recently become engaged to Sasha Liebowitz.

I know I said a great many things to you, and I meant everything I said at the time. I was absolutely sincere in my feelings for you.

I know you are now extremely upset with me, and I'm sorry I hurt you.

I hope one day you may be able to forgive me.

Apologetically,

Levi

Two weeks later, on a Sunday morning, the doorbell rang in Bushkin's apartment. Sasha answered the door.

"Is Levi in?" asked Sonia, who was wearing the heart he gave her.

"He's not in."

"I'll wait for him."

"I would appreciate it if you wouldn't. Give me a number where he can reach you."

"I'm not leaving until I see him," said Sonia, who stood in the doorway.

"Please go," said Sasha, as she tried to close the door, but was unable to because Sonia was wedged in the doorway and pushed against the door with her weight and arms.

Sonia and Sasha began shouting at each other, until Levi appeared in their view.

"Let's leave, Sonia, so we can talk," Levi said.

As the two exited, Sasha became visibly upset and distraught.

Sonia and Bushkin went to a nearby restaurant and sat down.

"Do you want anything to eat?" Levi asked her.

"No. What happened, Levi? All the things you told me. The plans we made."

"I really can't explain it except to say that I think I've made the right decision."

"Then it's absolutely over between us, Levi?"

"Yes."

"Why couldn't you have at least called me?"

"I was embarrassed and ashamed."

"You know you really hurt me, Levi."

"I didn't mean to."

"But you have. Here, Levi," said Sonia, as she pulled the heart from her neck and slammed it on the table. "I hope you put it to better use the next time."

As Sonia walked out, Levi stared at the heart. He got up to follow her. He saw her disappear around the corner and took a step in her direction. Then he stopped and stood motionless.

He decided not to follow her but to return instead to the restaurant to retrieve the heart. When he went back to the table where they sat, the heart was missing. He asked the busboy if he saw it. The busboy said "no."

"I hope you put it to better use than I did," he said to the busboy, who smiled at him sheepishly.

When he returned to the apartment, Sasha was waiting for him apprehensively.

"Are we still together?" she asked fearfully.

"Of course. But I didn't want to hurt her. I did a lousy thing, a rotten, horrible thing. Here I am lecturing everyone on how to behave, and I'm just as bad as everyone else."

"No you're not, darling."

"Oh, yes I am," he said as he left the room.

Sasha followed him to the bedroom, and she put her arms around him.

"Look, Levi, none of us can undo the past. Mistakes were made. Let's look to the future. We have what we want: each other."

"I didn't want to hurt her, Sasha. Really, I didn't want to hurt her. Let me be alone. I'm going to take a walk and try to sort things out. I'm sorry."

"Are you sure we're still together?"

"I'm sure, Sasha. Good-bye."

Bushkin returned an hour later.

"Are you okay?" asked Sasha.

"Yes, let's plan the wedding."

"That's what I wanted to hear, darling. You've made me very happy."

"I'm as happy as you, Sasha. I love you. But I'm sorry over what I did."

"You'll get over it."

"I know, and so will she, but I did the wrong thing.

"When shall we be married, Sasha?"

"April, when the weather turns warmer."

"Where?"

"At the synagogue, Levi."

"How many people?"

"Roughly two hundred, consisting of friends, co-religionists and co-workers.

"Who will marry us, Levi?"

"We should have a new rabbi in place by the time of the ceremony, and Yakov Potemkin will be the best man. Who will be your maid of honor?"

"Tatyana Samuelson. How about ushers, Levi?"

"Amos Sephard and Isadore Samonovich. Who will be your bridesmaid, Sasha?"

"Sarah Potemkin, and Rachel Potemkin will be the flower girl, and Joshua Potemkin will be the ring bearer."

"Sasha, where do you want to go for our honeymoon?"

"Italy."

"What cities?"

"Venice, Florence and Rome, Levi."

A few days later, Isadore Samonovich called Bushkin at his apartment. "Our committee is ready with a preliminary report on the search for a new rabbi. I want to discuss this with you. When can we meet?"

"How about Wednesday night?"

"I'll see if the other members are available. Levi, you sound like you're having second thoughts."

"Well, not exactly. But it's time to move on. Yes, definitely, it's time to move on and for me to pursue some other interests."

"Like what?"

"Like writing. Say, maybe Sasha could be added to the committee."

"Why, to protect your interest?"

"Not exactly. Look, I've put my heart and soul in this. I want to make sure we have an appropriate successor."

"Levi, if Sasha is added to the committee, it will need the approval of the other committee people."

"I understand. Isadore, let's say we meet at 7:30 p.m. at the synagogue, and I will bring Sasha."

"It's 7:30, unless you hear differently from me."

At the meeting, Bushkin asked the committee if Sasha could be added to the group in order to screen the applications and make a recommendation to the board of directors. The committee agreed.

Next, Isadore Samonovich told the gathering of Yetta Samonovich and Amos Sephard, the two who, along with him, formed the original search committee, and Bushkin and Sasha, that fifteen applications had been received for the position of rabbi.

Bushkin suggested to help differentiate the candidates, all applying should be required to write an essay of three hundred words on: "How you would approach the position of Rabbi at the Ugograd Hebrew Congregation." Isadore suggested the essays be screened by the committee, which would include all present, and the two or three best would be brought in for interviews. The final decision would be based on the essay, interview, references, and the applicant's experience.

Bushkin asked if he could be included in the interview process. The committee unanimously concurred.

Isadore said all applicants will be given two weeks to submit essays, and each would be made fully aware of the problems that face the congregation.

When the essays arrived and were reviewed, one, from Anna Blumenthal, an associate rabbi from London, England, stood out.

She wrote:

Dear Mr. Samonovich,

I continue to be interested in the position of rabbi of the Ugograd Hebrew Congregation.

In conformance with your request, enclosed please find my essay.

The Melding of Secularism and Judaism in the Modern World

Judaism must evolve; yet it must retain its heritage and identity.

Judaism's heritage and basis for prayer will serve as our foundation, if I became rabbi. Yet, too, I won't be constrained by the past but I will be respectful of it.

My services will include the basic prayers, blessings, Torah and Haftarah readings. Yet my approach to my position will include a reaching out to all things Jewish: our music, literature, art, philosophy, and our accomplishments and failures.

I will try to view our commonality as Jews. I will not run from words like stereotype. Rather, I will try to understand what makes us like we are.

Too, I won't be naive. There is a wide secular world that can be irrational and dangerous to Jews, as history has many times taught us. We can't ignore the wider world, nor can we be hostage to it. Rather, we must understand it but retain what we are--our Jewishness is important as is our understanding, growth and evolution.

It is the melding of these elements that would define any rabbinate of which I am a part. My Jewish world is all encompassing and won't exist in a vacuum. My door will always be open to my congregation, which I will view as my extended family, my mishpachah.

I look forward to serving you.


When the committee again reviewed the qualifications of Anna Blumenthal and read her essay, the members knew they wanted to interview her immediately.

Rabbi Blumenthal came to Ugograd and met with the committee: Isadore and Yetta Samonovich, Amos Sephard and Sasha Liebowitz. Bushkin, as agreed, was present.

"Rabbi Blumenthal," said Samonovich, "I read your essay and went over your qualifications. Do you think, knowing our history and membership, you can be comfortable here?"

"Yes."

"Do you think you can get your message across?"

"Yes."

"How?"

"My door will always be open. My message will come across in study groups, sermons and meetings. I'm passionate about how I view things--not dogmatic, but passionate. I want to talk, study and evolve with my congregation. Ugograd was once a great Jewish mecca and can be again. I feel with the synagogue and the foundation laid by the membership and Levi Bushkin, as a part-time rabbi, we can make a difference and be in the vanguard of a continuing religious and Jewish intellectual evolution."

"Sasha, Amos, Yetta, Levi," said Isadore, "do you have any questions?"

"No," they said collectively.

"Rabbi Blumenthal, we'll be in touch with you shortly."

"What do you think?" asked Isadore. "Levi, your opinion first."

"I'll go along with what the group thinks."

"I think she's perfect," Amos said. "She's bright, enthusiastic, and she's much better looking than Levi."

"I think she'll be approachable and a friend," said Sasha. "She's a real person, not someone who will hold herself out like a self-anointed marble deity. I like her."

"I'm impressed," said Isadore. "I'm around people enough to know who's for real and who isn't.

"As you know, I've checked her considerable references, and she comes highly recommended. Yetta, what do you think?"

"I move the committee recommend her to the board of directors as our new rabbi."

"All in favor," said Isadore, "say 'Aye.'"

"Then it's unanimous," said Isadore. "The vote carries, 4-0. I will contact Rabbi Blumenthal to indicate that we will recommend her to the board and her approval should be a mere formality at this point."

As expected, at the next board of directors meeting, Anna Blumenthal was approved and hired as the rabbi. Isadore Samonovich advised her that tenure would begin March 1.

The congregation gave her a reception and an open house on Wednesday evening, and reporter Olga Tereshnova of the <u>Informant</u> and a photographer from the paper were also present. When Bushkin saw Tereshnova interview Anna, he walked over afterwards and said, "Olga can't always be trusted. Sometimes she has ulterior motives."

"Thank you, Levi," she replied, "but I will make my own mind up."

"I'm just trying to be helpful," he said as he walked away.

She conducted her first service on a Friday night in March. During the sermon, she said, "We are not considered a racial type. Yet we can have distinct looks and we are called a Semitic people.

"We are considered like other people, but someone once said when you have two Jews, you have three opinions.

"But what separates us: our looks--at times; our argumentation--all too often; but there's something deeper. As a people we are defined by our souls. To have a Jewish soul makes us different. It makes us charitable (tzedakah), humane, and caring. It makes us pursue the fine arts, literature, music, education and other intellectual pursuits.

"Read a book by a Jewish author--an Arthur Miller, an Aharon Appelfeld, a Budd Schulberg, a Bernard Malamud. Listen to the music of a Jewish composer--a Leonard Bernstein, a George Gershwin, an Arnold Schoenberg or a Gustav Mahler. Listen, feel it, grasp it. There is something wonderful about it and absorbing to it.

"Often in these pursuits new ground is broken and novel dimensions attained. And then there is that feeling--that expression that can only come from within.

"That's what makes us unique and different. That's what defines us.

"As your rabbi, I want you to know during my tenure my door is always open. My home is your home and I hope vice versa. This synagogue is our synagogue. If you see me on the street, invite me in for tea; or I'll have you over for a Shabbos' dinner and we can walk to shul. We can talk about anything you wish: from the topics raised in tonight's sermon to anything you desire.

"This is my message, and you are my congregation.

"Amen."

"Before we conclude the service, I would like to announce it will be my mitzvah to marry Dr. Sasha Liebowitz and your former rabbi, Levi Bushkin, next month.

"Following the service, there will be an Oneg Shabbat, where I'd like to meet any of the congregants whom I haven't already met.

"We will close tonight's service with Odon Olam."

At the Oneg Shabbat, several of the congregants approached Bushkin to say how pleased they were with his successor. He became wistful. Meanwhile, as Anna greeted the congregants at the Oneg Shabbat, she seemed to fill the room by the dint of her personality.

"Levi, you're pouting," said Sasha.

"No I'm not," he snapped.

She began to laugh hysterically.

"You big ham, you big, stupid ham. What do you think you were when you were on the bemah, God's right-hand man? The beginning and end of Jewish wisdom? At times you are, unintentionally, the funniest person I've ever met."

"Am I really acting silly?"

"Like a big baby. Let go. Stop it. You did a good thing, stepping down when you did. We have a good person in your stead."

"Sasha."

"What is it now, Levi?"

"Do you think she'll let me fill in when she goes on vacation?"

"Levi."

"Just kidding, Sasha. Just kidding."

"Are you?"

# Chapter XXIV

## Sasha: Such a Beautiful Bride, Such a

## Shayne Punim

The day of the wedding, those in the procession were required to arrive early.

"Amos," said Joshua Potemkin, "can we talk?"

"Sure, boychik. What do you have to say?"

"You know, Amos, in a few years I'm going to be bar mitzvahed. I figure I will take in a lot of cash. Maybe we can buy some cabs together."

"It's a tough business, boychik. The drivers can be unreliable and they can steal from you."

"Well, if we buy the cabs together, I'm going to have to learn the business, and the sooner the better. Maybe I can work for you in the summer."

"What would you do?"

"I could keep the books."

"I have a bookkeeper, but I need someone to keep the place orderly, assist the mechanic and sweep up."

"Amos, that's not what I had in mind. I was thinking more in terms of an executive position."

"Boychik, like I said, I need someone to clean up. Besides, maybe you're better off keeping your bar mitzvah money in the bank."

"No, the bank isn't for me."

"Joshua, how about the stock market?"

"Well, my father says if you want to invest, you're better off buying the major indexes. He says most of the money managers can't beat the indexes. He says for most of these money managers to earn big bucks is nothing but a racket. In fact, my father says it's a bigger racket than what he does."

"I see. Tell me, what does your sister think?"

"What does she know? She plays the piano."

"Oh."

"My mother thinks she has real talent, but I can't see it. Every time we have guests over, my mother always shows her off and lets her play. I sit there with a fake smile and pretend I'm enjoying it. To tell you the truth, I feel like screaming.

"Do you know what else my mother does?"

"What?"

"She's always schlepping us to some concert or opera. The opera is the worst--all that yelping and squealing in a language you can't understand. I don't get it. How people can listen to that stuff with a straight face is beyond me."

"What does your father think?"

"He sleeps through the opera. But if he starts snoring too loudly, my mother pokes him and he wakes up. Then he falls off again."

"How about your sister and mother?"

"They actually seem to like it. Then again, I can't figure those two out."

"Do you like the concerts any better?"

"Nothing is as bad as the opera. However, I tried to explain to my mother if we could get a tape of the selection and listen to it at home, it would be cheaper than buying four tickets. She told me because my sister is so talented, it's best if she observes the piano soloist playing with the orchestra. Then I said, 'I don't see where she's all that talented.' That did it. The next thing I know is that she grabs a coat hanger and starts chasing me all over the house, and she's screaming at me like a meshugena."

At that moment, Sarah Potemkin came over and said, "Joshua, it's time to take your position in the procession. The wedding will soon begin."

"Mom."

"What is it, Joshua?"

"Can I tell Amos my latest idea?"

"Never mind, I'll tell him."

"Did you hear, Amos, he wants to tear down the synagogue and put up a parking garage with stores on the ground level.

"I always wanted a son who would be a doctor, a scientist, a professor; instead, I'll say do you know who my son is? They'll say no, Sarah, who is he? I'll say, why, he's Joshua Potemkin, the parking lot king!"

"Joshua."

"What is it, Mom?"

"Please watch what you're eating. We had a hard time fitting you in a tuxedo."

"Mom."

"What is it, Joshua?"

"I'm hungry."

"Amos."

"What Sarah?"

"Do you have two aspirin?"

"No, but Tatyana might."

As the wedding procession began, and Irena Goldsmith of the Ugograd Symphony began to play,

Tatyana Samuelson, the maid of honor, accompanied Yakov Potemkin, the best man, down the aisle.

"Look at Tatyana's dress," said one of the guests.

"What about it?" another replied.

"It's nice, but she'll never wear it again."

Sarah Potemkin, the bridesmaid, was accompanied by ushers Amos Sephard and Isadore Samonovich, who flanked her.

Next came the flower girl, Rachel Potemkin, and the ring bearer, her brother, Joshua, who accompanied her.

"Look at Rachel, a real shayne mayd'l," said one of the guests.

"She got all the looks in that family," said another.

Meanwhile, Joshua, as he walked down the aisle, waved to the guests.

Levi Bushkin followed.

Then Irena Goldsmith began the Wedding March of Felix Mendelssohn and Sasha appeared.

"Such a shayne punim," said a guest. "She's magnificent," said another. "She's so gorgeous, she should be in the movies," chimed yet another. "Levi's got himself a beautiful bride."

She joined Levi under the chupah with Rabbi Blumenthal and the couple took their vows.

He broke the glass with a stomp of his right foot, then he passionately kissed Sasha. As man and wife they left the chupah and, arm in arm, walked down the aisle.

Throaty shouts of mazel tov greeted the two as they left the area where the marriage ceremony was performed. The couple then waited to receive their guests in the reception line. As Levi and Sasha stood side by side as man and wife, he asked her how she felt. "Relieved and wonderful," she said. "And how about you?"

"Married to a beautiful girl."

As the couple met the guests, Sasha received numerous compliments as her deep-seated beauty and off-white dress offered a stunningly beautiful combination.

After they finished greeting their guests, Sasha and Levi took their seats at the head table. Dinner was served.

Following dinner, the couple visited each table.

As the music played and dancers filled the floor, Amos Sephard approached Rabbi Blumenthal. "Do you want to dance?" he asked her.

"I'd be delighted."

"You know, I've never danced with a rabbi before."

"Why is that?"

"All the ones I've known had beards."

"Well, Amos, how are you enjoying your new experience?"

"Uh, it's divine, Rabbi."

"You know I'm in the phone book, Amos."

"Are you listed under R, for rabbi?"

"No, I'm under E, for eligible."

At that moment, Amos dipped Anna.

"You're light on your feet, Amos."

"It helps to be that way around here."

As Amos and Anna sat down, Joshua Potemkin approached her. "Rabbi Blumenthal, may I have this dance?"

"Certainly, Joshua."

As the two cavorted on the floor, Joshua said, "Rabbi Blumenthal, may I ask you something?"

"What is that?"

"Rabbi, how much do they pay you?"

"Joshua, that's between me and the congregation. Why do you ask?"

"Well, I figure if I have to attend services, I might as well get paid for it. I know all the prayers so I could be the rabbi."

"Your mother told me that when you get older you want to join your father's law firm."

"Well, I won't practice law on the Jewish holidays; I'll be here. Besides, my father says it's good to diversify."

"I see, Joshua."

"You know something else, Rabbi Blumenthal?"

"What is that?"

"I think we should tear down the synagogue and put up a parking garage with stores on the first floor."

"Where would we pray, Joshua?"

"We could pray anywhere. Besides, we could always try to get another synagogue building from the city. My father says the city is sitting on a lot of valuable real estate, but it doesn't know it. My father says the people that run the city are a bunch of dumb goyim."

"Joshua, that's not nice."

"Well, he says it all the time."

The musicians played a traditional Jewish song and the males hoisted Sasha, as she sat in a chair, and the guests danced around her. After more dancing, the bride and groom left to change. When they returned, she was dressed in a pink suit with a button-down jacket and a matching skirt. He wore a sports coat, slacks and a tie. After this appearance, during which they were introduced as Mr. and Mrs. Levi Bushkin, the couple left. The festivities continued for another hour.

As the newly married couple returned to their apartment, Levi asked Sasha, "How does it feel to be married?"

"Like I'm Mrs. Bushkin. How do you feel, Levi?"

"Happy. You know I fell in love with you from the minute I met you, although I didn't think there would be so many twists and turns until we got to this point."

"Frankly, Levi, there were many times I thought today would never come."

"Are you happy it came?"

"Yes, darling. When you fell in love with me, I fell in love with you."

"Sasha, tomorrow we will wake up and fly to Italy. Let's enjoy ourselves."

"When you wake up tomorrow, I will have a surprise for you."

"Can you tell me now?"

"Let it wait until tomorrow."

As the couple went to bed, Sasha said, "Hold me." He did, and the couple fell asleep in each other's arms.

As they awoke the following morning, Levi said, "Mrs. Bushkin, can you tell me what your surprise is?"

"Wait until we're on the plane."

"Yes, Mrs. Bushkin."

As the plane took off for Italy, Levi asked, "Mrs. Bushkin, can you now tell me your surprise?"

"You're going to be a father."

"What!"

"You heard me."

"My God, when did you find out?"

"Two weeks ago."

"Why did you keep it a secret?"

"I wanted to surprise you. The baby should come in January."

"Sasha, should we end the honeymoon now so you can go back and rest?"

"Don't be ridiculous."

"Have you thought about names?"

"No, Levi."

"We will have to decorate one of the bedrooms for our son."

"How do you know it will be a boy?"

"It has to be."

"Suppose it's a girl."

"Then she'll have to be as beautiful as her mother."

In Venice the couple strolled along the canals.

"Venice must have been the commercial center of the world," Levi said to Sasha. "Look how these tall buildings, for their time, crowd up to the water's edge. This had to be the place."

Later, the couple observed the Jewish ghettoes of Venice.

"The Jews, the stepchildren of history," said Levi. "For so long no permanent home: rounded up here; herded there; almost always rootless. The state's non-citizens. Use, segregate, and discard--almost always the story of the Jews."

"Why do we always need a history lesson, Levi? Can't we just enjoy ourselves?"

"I'm sorry."

The couple made their way to St. Mark's Square and walked the area. Then the Bushkins had dinner at a trattoria. "Are you enjoying yourself, Sasha?" Bushkin asked.

"Yes, Italy is beautiful. I enjoy watching the people. They seem to live for the moment, unconcerned about what tomorrow might bring."

"I wish I could be more that way," replied Levi. "I wish I didn't take myself so seriously."

"I think it's your nature to always be contemplative and on edge."

"Maybe when the baby comes, I'll loosen up."

"I hope so."

"By the way, how is Baby Bushkin today?"

"Baby and Mother Bushkin are doing fine. How is Daddy Bushkin?"

"So long as mother and child are doing well, Daddy Bushkin is fine. Tomorrow we will take the train to Florence. What do you want to do today, Sasha?"

"How about if we see the Doges' Palace, and then we will walk on the Rialto Bridge?"

"Fine. Did you check with Baby Bushkin?"

"The baby has no choice but to go along."

After the Bushkins finished touring for the day and sat in a restaurant, Levi said to Sasha, "The Italians were the master builders. The scale, the details, the plazas, it is astonishing."

On the train the next day to Florence, Bushkin asked Sasha how she liked Venice.

"It is the most unique place I've ever been to, but I'm really looking forward to seeing Florence again."

"Me too."

As they toured Florence, they saw Ghiberti's doors and toured the Uffizi Museum and the Pitti Palace. The synagogue, as a result of the Holocaust, was closed, but the Bushkins viewed its distinct oriental style from the outside. As they did, they said little. They didn't have to. Each could feel the other's despair.

The following day, they saw Michelangelo's David. Sasha became visibly distraught.

"I remember seeing this with my fiance, Yuri. Please hold me."

"Are you okay, Sasha?"

"I'll be all right. Maybe we better leave."

"I understand."

Outside the building she said, "You know you remind me so much of Yuri. Although there were times he, like you, could be very difficult to be around, you are so similar to him: honest, direct, committed…a real mentsch."

"Why does everything have to take such distorted twists and turns, Sasha?"

"That's the eternal question I'll never answer, Levi."

"Neither will I. Look, Sasha, as long as we have each other and the baby," he said, with a smile, "everything will be fine."

"You're right, Levi."

"Sasha, let's go back to the hotel, relax, and then we will go out to dinner. Remember, you and the baby will need rest."

"Believe it or not, I'm not the first person to ever go through pregnancy."

"We don't want to take chances, Sasha."

During dinner that evening, Bushkin said to Sasha, "You know it is obvious to me a reason for the poverty of the Middle Ages is that there was too much time and capital allocated to church building. Perhaps if the people would have had less-grand churches, they could have had better housing, nutrition, medical care, and clothing."

"What should we do tomorrow, Levi?"

"How about if we take a walk along the Arno River, grab a bite to eat, and decide then."

"You're the tour guide."

"Maybe the outdoor market is a good idea. I'm told there are some extraordinary bargains there."

A day later, the couple boarded a train and went to Rome, the last leg of their three-city tour. There they saw the ceiling of the Sistine Chapel. As Bushkin and Sasha looked up at the painted ceiling, he asked her, "Do you think Michelangelo could have been from this earth?"

"It's astonishing, Levi. Whatever perfection is, he took it to a new level. Somehow, he's better than perfect."

"My sentiments exactly, Sasha. Whenever I see something he did, all I do is stare in amazement. Would you want to see the Moses?"

"The last time I was here I saw it with Yuri. To see it again will make me sad."

"I understand, darling."

Later that day they toured the Colosseum. As they walked inside, Bushkin said to Sasha, "The scale that these people built on totally amazes me. They were the masters. They must have been so far ahead of their time, that the gap between them and everybody else had to be hard to define."

"You have an opinion on everything, don't you, Levi?"

"You want my opinion on you?"

"It depends if it's good or bad."

"How about honest?"

"Okay."

"You're beautiful and you're everything I ever wanted, and when Baby Bushkin comes, I hope he looks just like you."

"Suppose Baby Bushkin is a girl?"

"Then she better look like you."

"That was sweet," said Sasha, laughing. "What should we do tomorrow?"

"Maybe a little shopping and touring."

"Fair enough, Levi."

The following day they toured the Appian Way and the Catacombs. After some shopping, the two had dinner and retired for the evening.

The next day they awoke, had breakfast, and went to the airport to return to Ugograd. "Did you enjoy yourself, Sasha?"

"Italy was like a fairy tale; I'm sorry we have to return home."

"Sasha, when the baby comes, that will be leg two of the fairy tale."

# Chapter XXV

## The Last Jew

Sasha was in her third month of pregnancy.

"You seem restless, Levi, and on edge."

"Well, I started it."

"What?"

"My novel."

"Why didn't you tell me?"

"I told you when I ended my tenure as rabbi, I was going to begin writing."

"I didn't think it would be so soon."

"The first chapter is nearly finished. You'll read it and give me your opinion."

"Sure."

"I'll have it finished in the next week or so."

"I want to read it as soon as it's completed."

Bushkin picked up his recently started manuscript and began reading it.

<u>The Last Jew</u>
by Levi Bushkin

The two security guards stood outside the shul. "Did you see Mr. Bushkin come in today?" one asked the other.

"No, maybe we should go inside and check."

"Mr. Bushkin, wake up," said the security guard as he shook him.

"He's not responding. Call the doctor."

The doctor soon came and called for an ambulance. Prior to his being loaded on the ambulance, he expired and the doctor pronounced him dead. The security guard called a local priest, whom Bushkin had befriended, and gave him the instructions he had left. The instructions said Bushkin was to be given a Jewish burial in the cemetery outside the shul. The money for the stone and the burial was to be withdrawn from Bushkin's account. The other funds were to be used to turn the shul into a Jewish museum.

The priest then read a eulogy that reflected Bushkin's thoughts:

"He is thought to be the last Jew. The extinction of his people always worried him. But because of war, inquisition, pogrom, holocaust, and abandonment of faith, Mr. Bushkin is thought to be the last of his religion--the last of the children of Israel.

"As we lay him to rest, we end, so far as we know, a remarkable journey that began with Abraham and ended with Abraham Bushkin.

"I will now read, at Mr. Bushkin's request, the Kaddish: 'Yit-ga-dal ve-yit-ka-dash sh-mei ra-ba. . . .'"

As the priest finished the Kaddish, Bushkin was lowered into the ground.

A reporter from a local paper, Marina Shubin, who was assigned the story, asked the priest about Bushkin.

"Abraham Bushkin," she was told, "was the son of Levi and Sasha Bushkin. He was, like his father, a professor of literature. Years ago, he wrote several novels, but they are out of print.

"He lived to be ninety. In his later years, he came to shul every day to study, write and record his memoirs. You will find his material in the numerous file cabinets in the office. Knowing Mr. Bushkin, everything is impeccably chronicled."

The young reporter, with the approval of the priest, entered the shul and began to sift through his personal effects. After several hours, Marina knew she had the makings of not only a remarkable series of articles but a book as well.

She met with her editor to discuss possible projects. Her editor was interested.

She returned to the shul and picked up a novel Bushkin had published forty years before. She found his words haunted her. It was his descriptions. His empathy. His humanity. It was as if they were kindred spirits, compadres of the soul. She went through a file and looked at his pictures. She saw his features were like hers, Semitic. As she studied his features, Marina saw parts of herself as if she were a reflection in a mirror. She began to feel mesmerized and eerie.

"I didn't know Abraham Bushkin," she said to herself, "but there is something I feel. I read him and I feel he is talking to me. I see him as I look at myself. Am I a Jew?" she asked herself.

She went to City Hall and began to research genealogical records. Marina learned both sets of her grandparents were Jewish. Apparently, she felt, her parents must have abandoned their faith out of fear. She was raised without religion.

Marina returned to the shul regularly over the next several weeks and began to research and write her newspaper story, while simultaneously outlining her book. Meanwhile, she wrestled with her conscience. As she made her visits to the synagogue, Marina began to spend more and more time with the prayer books, and began to teach herself Hebrew. She asked herself: "Am I God's messenger? Am I a chosen one--a female Moses, an Abraham? Am I a link, a spirit of renewal and rebirth?"

The first of her newspaper installments was completed.

Abraham Bushkin: In Memoriam
by Marina Shubin

Abraham Bushkin was supposed to be the last of them--the last Jew. I never met him. I was unfamiliar with his novels. I didn't know what he looked like.

I went to his funeral. My interest was in recreating his story for my newspaper. I began to read a novel he wrote called the European Rhapsody. The protagonist was Avrum Schifman. He was a beautiful man, but not without fault. He wanted to do the right thing by people, even when this went against his self-interest.

When his foil, Moshe Rifkin, berates him for his "naivete," Schifman replies, "I'm serving my self interest by doing right."

Eventually, Schifman loses his possessions; his wife leaves him and his children disassociate themselves from him.

"You naive fool," Rifkin tells him, "you could have had it all."

"But I do," replies Schifman, "my conscience is clear, my soul is pure, and those who deserted me made me understand that no matter how difficult things become, goodness always transcends evil. Evil may prevail, but one is at peace so long as the soul is pure. In the end he tells Rifkin, "It is I who am the happy one. Are you?"

I interviewed some of his students. They remembered him for his insight and how he prodded their imagination and feelings. They enjoyed his class and his repartee. One said, "He pushed us to think and interpret, and we responded. He challenged our intellects and we were, in every sense of the word, his students. He was a hard grader but a fair man, and very approachable. Inside the classroom he was demanding; outside he was your friend."

I find I have much in common with this man. I don't know: Was he the last Jew? How many of you have Jewish roots and don't know it? I read Abraham Bushkin's work and became attached. I looked at his pictures, and I saw my features duplicated. In a sense, I looked into his soul and listened. And then my soul says: He is like you. Then who am I? I thought I knew. Now I need to find out. But I knew this: Abraham Bushkin isn't the last Jew. If you suspect you have Jewish roots, write, call or email me.

Before she had the article printed, Marina took it to her editor for approval.

"It's quite different," he told her," let me run it by the editor-in-chief."

When the editor-in-chief reviewed it, he referred the piece to his publisher who said, "Run it. Maybe it will boost circulation."

The article appeared with Abraham Bushkin's picture. Astonishingly, Marina Shubin received five hundred responses.

She then asked her respondents, via mail, if they wanted to meet in a public forum and arranged to do so in the newspaper's auditorium.

Two hundred and fifty people attended.

Marina began to talk about her experience and her article, as well as the book she planned to write.

She closed her talk with the following statement: "Prior to Abraham Bushkin's funeral, I looked in the mirror and saw who I thought I was. I now look in the mirror and know I need to find out who and what I really am.

"Abraham Bushkin, a man I never knew, now communicates with me via his novels, other writings and through my interviews with his students.

"My soul clings to his, and my spirit is attached to him. Spiritually, I find I'm a Jew."

Marina paused and then invited questions from the audience. After the question-and-answer session, she was approached by Stepan Zavadinsky.

"Ms. Shubin," he said, "I want to talk to you about your writing and research. Would you have dinner with me one evening?"

"Yes."

"How about tomorrow night?"

"Can you pick me up at the newspaper?"

"I'll be there."

As the two sat in the restaurant, Zavadinsky said to her, "I felt something when you spoke. It's hard to express my feelings except to say I have empathy for your words. The next time you go to Mr. Bushkin's synagogue, may I join you?"

"Sure. Abraham Bushkin has become my obsession, and Judaism may be my link to him."

"How about if I pick you up Saturday morning?"

"I will meet you. Here is my address."

As the two drove to the synagogue, Stepan said, "Marina, people tend to grow far larger in death than they were in life."

"I understand that."

"Are you sure you're not going through an obsessive infatuation?"

"I think it's far deeper than that."

As the two entered the synagogue, Marina gave Stepan one of Bushkin's novellas. He read portions of it as she continued to do research.

Several hours later, the two left the building.

"What do you think?" Marina asked him.

"Oh, he is a compelling writer, but I don't have the same reaction you have. Spiritually I'm unmoved."

"Do you want to return to the shul with me?"

"I don't think so."

"Well, I'm committed to my research. My soul says continue to probe."

As Bushkin completed Chapter I, he gave the manuscript to Sasha. She read it carefully.

"What do you think?" he asked her.

"It's very creative and eerie. I'm wondering if it's a distant mirror."

# Chapter XXVI

# Doubt!

Sasha was in her sixth month of pregnancy. The sex of the baby had been determined. It was a boy!

"Will he be a doctor or a writer?" Levi would continually joke to her.

"Let him always be happy," was her continual reply.

One day after he posed his almost-daily question, Sasha told Levi, "I'm scared."

"About what?"

"About the world we live in. We have been through an unprecedented horror. We have an obligation to our son, and to hopefully his offspring, to provide a safe environment."

"What are you suggesting?"

"That we move away from here and blend in somewhere else. We can change our names and alter our features. No one has to know we're Jews. The baby will never have to know."

"It's out of the question, Sasha."

"Would you be happy to know when we're deceased the 'mob' marches up the steps to take him, or his children, or their children?"

"You can't run, Sasha. We are what we are."

"Yes, but I'm a mother to be. There is nothing more important than the welfare of my son and hopefully,

267

God willing, my grandchildren and great grandchildren."

"Sasha, we will stay here and raise the baby in a Jewish household. Besides, when the mob comes, it's amazing how they know who is and who isn't. There is an old dictum: 'You can run but you can't hide.' We will always know who and what we are."

Following the conversation with Levi, Sasha made an appointment to see Rabbi Anna Blumenthal, a week later.

"So nice to see you, Sasha. You're carrying beautifully. I know how excited you and Levi must be."

"I'm scared, Anna. Scared about the future. I'm frightened of the climate. I have a responsibility to my son, and hopefully to his children, to avoid, as much as possible, a mob coming up the steps one day to take him away because he observes the Jewish faith. My son comes first."

"In religion, Sasha, we're taught the spirit can be powerful and do wonderful things."

"In all due respect, Rabbi, I've seen, in my time, too many well-meaning 'spirits' crushed because of that attitude. In medicine we're taught to minimize risks and maximize outcomes."

"Sasha, in a balanced life there is a proper melding of the spiritual and scientific world."

"Anna, what good is the spirit against the mob?"

"Sasha, I heard how Father Vagins stood up against the mob on the anniversary of our congregation moving into the synagogue. How he told those criminals 'Before you touch any of my Jewish brothers, you will crucify me first on these synagogue steps.' And how his actions defused the mob."

"Rabbi, if the world were made up of people like Father Vagins and you, we wouldn't be having this discussion. The world isn't a Garden of Eden.

"Did you know one of the leaders of the murderous mob was the anti-Semite Alexander Shukov, whom I had saved in surgery?

"I thought about letting him die, but I couldn't do it. Yet I always had a premonition that the day would come when he would try to murder me. And he did. And I have to expose my son to this insanity. I tell you, Rabbi, I don't want my son to confront any more cruelty than he will have to."

"What does Levi say?"

"Did you know Levi is writing a novel?"

"I didn't."

"It is as if he is saying the Jews will never die. In many respects the novel is quite eerie, quite revealing and remarkably compelling."

"Why?"

"It depicts our son, Abraham Bushkin, who dies at the age of ninety, as the last Jew. The funeral is covered by a reporter, Marina Shubin, who discovers she has Jewish roots and, upon discovering her origins, begins a period of change along with others who discover they, too, have a Jewish ancestry. As a group, they begin to probe and confront change. Marina is at first drawn to Abraham Bushkin, who, like his father, is a professor of literature, by his Semitic features, which are like hers. When she sees Bushkin's picture, Marina sees 'parts of herself, as if she were a reflection in a mirror.' She reads a novel he wrote and is drawn by his empathy and humanity. She and Abraham are kindred spirits and, 'compadres of the soul.'

"Though raised without religion, she begins to see Judaism as a link to our son. She begins to teach herself Hebrew and reviews prayer books. Marina meets with others, who also believe they have Jewish roots. Marina discusses their commonality and the feelings that are aroused in her when she is around people who suspect they have Jewish origins.

"Eventually, a nouveau Jewish movement forms, and she sees herself as something of a Messiah."

"Sasha, the novel sounds beautiful and compelling. It's when we understand who and what we are that we can do things like this book."

"Rabbi, I understand who I am: a doctor, a healer, and a Jew. I did a wonderful and humane thing when I saved the life of a Jew-killer, the anti-Semitic Alexander Shukov.

"I debated with myself, the night before I operated on him, whether I should save or kill him. I kept hearing the voice of my father, Daniel, who said, 'Jews don't act that way. Don't make me ashamed of you. Don't bring shame to your family.'

"When in surgery, my medical training and instincts took over and I saved him.

"My repayment: He almost murdered me."

"You're here, Sasha."

"Barely, Rabbi. After the confrontation with the anti-Semitic mob, do you know Levi insisted we walk back to his apartment. He told me he wants them to see us walk back and that they are just as afraid of us as we are of them. I said, 'Aren't you scared?' He said so much so that he hopes he 'doesn't urinate in his pants.'

He said, 'When you stand up to them, they won't know how to react, except as the cowards they really are.' Rabbi, I don't want my child forced into situations like that.

"You know, Rabbi, the most beautiful men in my life were my father, Daniel; my fiance, Yuri Fromkin; and now my husband, Levi. My father and Yuri were murdered. Their crimes: They were Jews. The only reason I survived was that I walked away from a crowd of three hundred at a camp. I expected to be shot. I didn't care. Everyone I knew had been murdered. Levi will tell you that if the war had lasted another day, he would have been murdered. By those margins we survived. This isn't life; this is madness. I will not, and cannot, subject my son to this, Rabbi. It's cruel and unfair to him."

"Sasha, you're a mother-to-be. Whatever decision you make, I'll respect. I'm very fond of you and Levi. I, too, wish life wasn't so cruel.

"Remember our Father, Abraham, faced the ultimate test of obedience, the sacrifice. He obeyed God and our faith survived."

"Mothers, Rabbi, don't have children to sacrifice."

After the meeting ended, Sasha returned home.

"You're home late, Sasha," Levi said. "Where were you?"

"I met with Rabbi Blumenthal."

"What did you discuss?"

"Oh, we just chatted."

"About what?"

"Your novel."

"And what else?"

"My fear of the future."

271

"What did she say?"

"She mainly listened."

"Were there any conclusions reached?"

"No. Mainly I needed someone to talk to."

"I see. Sasha, if we move away from here and disguise our identity, and the baby grows up and discovers his origins, what would you tell him?"

"I would tell him the truth."

"Remember, they tried to cover up Moses' identity."

"Sure, because the Pharaoh ordered all male Hebrew children killed. I want my baby to have a normal life."

"He will have a normal life here in our growing Jewish community. He will have the best education. He will be exposed to his co-religionists, and Jewish learning and institutions. And on his bar mitzvah day, he will read from the Torah!

"Maybe one day he'll become a great Jewish writer and we'll be so proud."

"And maybe one day they'll burn his book and throw him in an oven."

"Sasha, maybe we shouldn't talk about this now."

"If not now, when? The baby will be here in less than three months."

"Sasha, just try to relax for the next few days. Don't try to anticipate the future. We're lucky people. We're alive; we're healthy; and we will soon have a baby boy who will look just like his mother."

"Levi, you're my husband, but don't make me take the baby and run away."

"You're being irrational."

"Am I?"

"Look, let's stay calm and not do anything we will regret later."

"Levi, I'm sorry for how I feel, but I'm scared for our son."

"I understand. We will stay here as a family and live and love one another together."

"Maybe in a few days I'll get over this."

"Remember what your fiance Yuri told you: 'You can be scared but you can't be afraid.'"

"So they killed him, too. It's so hard to be a mother in times like this."

"Try for the time being to put this out of your mind."

"Maybe if you wouldn't have started that goddamn novel, I wouldn't have these feelings."

"If you want me to stop it, I will."

"No, I think it will be published and maybe it will become a classic.

"But those descriptions of our son, Abraham Bushkin, as the 'last Jew,' left me uneasy and on edge. It all seems so damn real. I'm having trouble sorting things out."

"Sasha, this weekend let's use Isadore Samonovich's cabin in the woods. Getting away from here could be the right thing. We can walk the nature trails and sit by the lake. You're thinking too much."

"Maybe I'm not thinking enough. I want to look to the future with optimism, but it's hard."

"When the baby comes, your mind will be absorbed with our child. You will have less time for such contemplation and that will be good."

"Maybe I'll have less time to think, but will the problems go away?"

"We will always have problems, but we will solve them together. Our commitment will be to our child. He will absorb our energies, so there will be less time to worry about things we can't control."

"Levi, are you going to take the book with you?"

"Yes, I'll do a little work on it, unless you mind."

"No, I enjoy reading it, but the descriptions of our son upset me."

"It's only fiction."

"Is it?"

"I'm not a soothsayer."

"But the plot has so many elements of reality, and the way you depict our son makes everything seem so plausible."

"What do you think of Marina Shubin?"

"I like her character, especially the way she feels for our son."

"Remember, our son stays the course. He is born and lives as a Jew. It is his empathy that so inspires Marina Shubin."

"I know and love that, but I'm scared."

At Isadore's cabin, Levi and Sasha awoke on a Saturday and ate breakfast. "Let's take a walk," Levi said to her. "There are some nice trails and the foliage is coming in beautifully."

As the couple walked along a trail, Sasha said, "It's so peaceful up here. Why is nature so beautiful and so many people so ugly?"

"There are beautiful people, too. And all of nature isn't so beautiful."

"That's true. What is Marina Shubin up to?"

"Oh, she thinks the world of our son. She's now writing a book about him. It depicts him as a sensitive author and human being whose words have outlived him."

"That makes me happy, Levi. Put your arm around me. What else is she up to?"

"What do you think she is up to?"

"I'm sure as her neo-Jewish movement develops, she upsets segments in society."

"She does. Irrational people will always be in our midst. But our son has touched her, and Marina, in turn, has touched others. It's a beautiful story.

"You see, even if we run away, Marina Shubin would have a hard time finding our son. So we will live in Ugograd, among our people, and make it easier for her."

"If life were only so simple, Levi."

"When the baby comes, life will be beautiful. I bet he's thinking about his first book now and is upset at us for talking so loudly and breaking his concentration. Shhh, Sasha, not so loud."

"Levi, you're the one who does all the yelling."

"That's because you do all the screaming. Shhh, Sasha, we don't want to make a bad impression on the baby."

"Oh, we'll do that when he's born. Let's, at least, fool him for a while."

"Let's get off the trail and walk down by the lake, Sasha. It's so beautiful down there."

As they walked close to the water, Sasha said, "You know, my fondest dreams would have been to have our families present at our son's birth. My father always wanted a grandson. He would have taken the child everywhere."

"When the baby comes you'll tell him all about your father."

"You know, Levi, no matter how old we get, we will never outgrow the guilt of being survivors."

"Maybe one day I'll write a book on that."

"I'm sure it would be a compelling read, but I hope our son will never have to know from any of this."

"He won't.

"Why don't we turn around, Sasha, and head back. Besides, you need your rest."

"If it were up to you, I'd never get out of bed. You'd be some obstetrician. You'd have a hundred patients, all bedridden."

"And if they were like you, I'm sure they would never listen."

"Sasha, this is good time we're spending together. Out here is like another world, it's easier to be at peace with yourself."

"Levi, when we get back we will still have to confront hard choices."

"No we won't. We are staying in Ugograd. We're not running. The baby will be raised as a Jew in a Jewish household. He will learn about Abraham, Moses, David, Solomon, David Ben Gurion and the State of Israel. He will be my son in every sense of the word."

"Levi, my opinion doesn't count?"

"Sure it counts. But I'm his father; he'll be raised as a Jewish male on my say so. We're staying in this community!"

"Levi, we can talk about this later."

"That's just it, we won't talk about this later. The case is closed."

"My feelings as a mother don't count?"

"Sure they count. You're the glue. You will nurture our son and love him. I will give him structure and teach him priorities and what is important.

"Sasha, please let's enjoy the rest of the time we have up here. Let's not be frightened of the future."

"Can you blame me?"

"No, but fear is no way to live. We are about to have a son. That's the most joyous thing that can happen to a man."

"But fear and hate are all around us. You found me in a mountain outside of Tashni, hiding for my life. I saved that son-of-a-bitch Alexander Shukov's life, and I was almost fired because of a letter I sent his wife. Then he and that mob marched up our synagogue steps with the intention of killing us. Everything is the Jews this and the Jews that. There is no peace. That book, that goddamn awful book, talks of our son as the last Jew. Then you want to do a memoir of a survivor. And all those dead people--parents, relatives and friends."

"So take the baby, Sasha, leave me and run away. Live in isolation. Live without roots. And one day the baby will grow up and realize he's different and will begin to ask you questions, then what will you say?"

"I'll tell him he's alive."

"Suppose they find out who he is and they take him away?"

"I'll tell him I tried, as only a mother could."

"Your family comes first, Sasha."

"My baby comes first, Levi."

"No more talk about this, Sasha. No more. This isn't healthy. This isn't constructive."

"But, Levi, it's so necessary."

# Chapter XXVII

## The Survivor, Father and Patriarch

He sat with a yellow writing pad in front of him. Levi's novel was two-thirds finished. But he wanted to write something different, even if he had to do it concurrently with the novel.

He was living as a survivor and wanted to reflect on that. He wrote the title: <u>A Jewish Survivor: A Personal Memoir</u> by Levi Bushkin.

He began to write:

Why was it necessary for me to be a survivor? Because I'm a Jew.

Why do people dislike Jews? To them it is fashionable, and we're an easy target.

Why the Jews? Who better to blame than a small and, at times, powerful, visible minority.

Then why do I have to be a survivor? Because irrational people forced me to be one. They sought my life when I never harmed them.

Is it deeper than that? No.

Will it ever be deeper than that? Of course not.

Will people ever change? I doubt it.

Why will people never change? Because they are easily led into an unthinking, destructive, conforming mass.

Then why do I want to go on? Because I love life and choose, against all odds, to be an optimist. To me, tomorrow will always be better than today.

Why am I an optimist? I have beautiful Sasha, the love of my life. We do so much together, and she is everything to me, as I hope I am to her. I was born to love her.

She is about to give birth to a beautiful baby boy, provided our son looks like her. She is what I always wanted: smart, beautiful, and, next to my son, the best thing that ever happened to me. With her, life is and will stay interesting. She has a mind of her own.

When we met, each of us had suffered grievous losses of friends, family, and she had lost her fiance. We settled in Ugograd and those early days were strange. When you walked the streets the people looked at you--Jewish survivors--either in contempt or shame. To our knowledge, we were the only Jews in a city that was once a hub of Jewish life. Sasha and I were immediately employed, and the fact of our employment prompted an article in the Informant newspaper's national edition. A small group of other survivors followed.

We wanted to live as Jews, in spite of the fact that we had recently been a hunted minority. We formed a small congregation and I became the rabbi, a position for which I was totally unprepared.

I began to feel something as I probed my soul like never before. My sense of spiritualism was remarkable. I reached out to my congregants. I knew we all felt something that transcended the immediacy of a service or minyan. It had to. We came before God, so few of us, so decimated by Holocaust, yet we were there. Instead of rejecting God, we embraced our faith.

Our original group was remarkably diverse.

At that moment, Sasha came into the room.

"Levi," she said.

"What is it, Sasha?"

"It's time. The baby is coming. My water broke."

"Oh my God. Let me call a cab." The two took the elevator to the lobby and waited for the cab.

By mistake, two cabs came. When Levi got in and said in a sharp, urgent voice, "University Hospital," the driver, not seeing Sasha standing on the curb, drove off without her as Levi closed the door as the vehicle sped off. From the rear window, he saw Sasha enter the second cab. Both cabs arrived simultaneously at the hospital. When Sasha exited the cab, she was placed in a wheelchair and was taken to a room.

Levi called Yakov Potemkin that Thursday evening at 6:15 to tell him Sasha had gone into labor, and he asked him to call the others. By 7:15 Tatyana Samuelson, Rabbi Anna Blumenthal, Amos Sephard, Yetta and Isadore Samonovich, Father Yosef Vagins, Yakov and Sarah Potemkin and their children, Joshua and Rachel, had joined Levi in the waiting room.

The group sat, waiting. Isadore Samonovich began pacing.

"What's the problem, Isadore?" Amos Sephard asked him.

"My shrink has increased at the store. It's killing my bottom line. I think we're in a recession. Each time the economy starts going bad, my sales start to decline and shrink increases. I don't need some economist to tell me we're in a recession. I know we're in one. If the people want to know what's happening with the economy, they should call me."

"Stop eating your heart out, Isadore," his wife Yetta told him. "We've been through this before."

"Yes," he replied, "but it's so aggravating."

"Maybe you should stop pacing and try to relax."

"I can't, Yetta. I can't."

"So keep pacing, Isadore, like that will make the problems go away."

"Amos," asked Rabbi Blumenthal, "you've never come to one of our study groups. Why?"

"To tell you the truth, Rabbi, I probably wouldn't feel that comfortable. I've had less formal education that the others, and what I've learned, I've learned the hard way, on the streets. I probably couldn't offer too much to the group."

"What do you like to do, Amos?"

"Mostly work and in my spare time I go to the fights."

"Did you know at one time there were a lot of Jewish world champions? There was Benny Leonard, Barney Ross and "Slapsie Maxie" Rosenbloom. Daniel Mendoza, a Sephardic Jew, was the English champion between 1791 and 1795."

"I didn't realize that, Rabbi."

"Do you ever read?"

"Just the newspapers--mainly the sports and business section."

"Aren't you limiting yourself?"

"Not really. If you follow the news' cycles over time, they tend to repeat themselves. It's mostly the corrupt politicians and the masses that follow like sheep. It's all a nonsensical bore to me."

"Aren't you being too cynical?"

"To tell you the truth, Rabbi, I don't think I'm being cynical enough. Look, I respect what you do, but sometimes your sermons are so naive, I cringe. When it comes to practical life, you're not a fountain of wisdom."

"I resent that, Amos."

"Why?"

"Because I do."

"Is that a good reason?"

"Well, no."

"Rabbi, do you know what's bulging under my sports coat?"

"No."

"It's a handgun. Do you know why I carry a handgun?"

"No."

"Because we continually handle cash. When you handle cash, you're a target for thieves."

"You wouldn't use the handgun, would you?"

"Sure, I almost used it last week. A mechanic pulled a knife on me. I told him if he takes another step forward, I would blow his brains out. So he dropped the knife."

"I don't believe you would have shot him."

"If he would have taken another step forward, I would have shot him through the head. Better him than me.

"That's why I hate it when people give me an impractical version of reality and morality."

"Amos, when we danced at Levi's wedding, you seemed to enjoy yourself. Didn't you find me attractive?"

"I did."

"I thought you would have called me by now."

"Rabbi, what could we have in common?"

"Maybe more than you could imagine."

"What are you doing Saturday night, Anna?"

"I'm free. How about you?"

"I'm going to the fights. Would you care to join me?"

"I'd be delighted."

"By the way," asked Father Vagins, "what will your sermon be on Friday night, Rabbi Blumenthal?"

"Oh, I'll probably talk on non-violent solutions in a violent world. I hate violence."

The adults in the room, after hearing her response, broke into collective hysterics.

"When you bring the baby home, Levi, I'd like to do a mural in his playroom," said Tatyana Samuelson.

"Tatyana," he replied, "do you think you could make it less significant than the ceiling on the Sistine Chapel?"

"What I have in mind is the baby ascending skyward towards a light, but he is continually blocked by a series of transparent panels. His journey represents the difficulty of life."

"Tatyana, can't you do something a little lighter, maybe something with some clowns?"

"How about if I do a series of headless clowns to represent a world in need of joy?"

"Tatyana, why don't you do a series of clowns holding up Atlas, who in turn is holding up the world. The mural will represent the power of joy, particularly the joy I'm feeling now."

"Whatever will make you happy, Levi."

"Tatyana, you should only know the happiness I'm feeling now."

"Mommy," said Joshua Potemkin. "I'm hungry."

"Here is some money. Rachel, go with your brother to the hospital cafeteria and make sure he doesn't overdo it."

"Yes, Mommy."

As the two sat in the hospital eatery and Joshua began to eat, he said, "Rachel, I've been thinking that I can make you a child star."

"How would you do that?"

"Well, I think you can sell the public anything. Last night I was watching TV and they had these four guys with guitars and a girl singer. The five of them looked like they hadn't had a bath in a month, and they couldn't play together or carry a tune. Meanwhile, the audience is jumping up and down like the Messiah has just come.

"Look, I figure we'll dress you up--maybe Isadore will give us a discount--and you'll smile at the right times, say the right things, and the public will eat you up."

"Joshua, I don't know if I'm ready."

"Listen to me, talent will have the least of anything to do with your success. Like I said, you can sell the public anything. Look, when you get right down to it, the people with all the talent--the opera singers, ballet dancers, and classical musicians--are the ones working for peanuts. Those who have the least talent are the ones making zillions of dollars. I figure if you play the piano with an orchestra, as long as you begin and end together, not too many people will know whether you flub a note or two in between.

"By the way, we will have to get a lawyer to represent us."

"Won't you use Daddy?"

"No, he'll want to be a partner and start to butt in. The last time I was in shul, I heard some guy say 'Yakov is always sticking his nose in everyone's business.' By the time he finishes with us, he'll be running everything."

"Joshua, who will be our lawyer?"

"There are thousands of lawyers. If you open the phone book, the listings of the lawyers take up the most space.

"You know practically everything the lawyers need is in form books. Daddy's office is loaded with them."

"If we don't use Daddy, Joshua, he'll be upset."

"We'll give him some consulting work to keep him happy. We can't let him run wild."

"But Mommy will be mad with us."

"I'll handle her. After the money starts rolling in, we'll get her something special. You know she'll be so grateful, she'll start crying, hug us and tell us how proud she is of her children.

"Let's see, Rachel, my fee will be thirty percent of the gross."

"How come so much?"

"Somebody has to run things. Let's get back."

When they returned, Sarah asked Rachel, "Did your brother watch his eating?"

"No, Mommy, he stuffed himself with candy."

"That does it, Rachel. You've lost your manager. You are on your own."

"Rachel, what is he talking about?"

"He says he's going to put me in show business, but when we use a lawyer, we'll have to use someone other than Daddy because he'll butt in and try to run things. He said Daddy would 'run wild.'"

"W-h-a-t? Vey iz mir," said Sarah.

"Levi," said Father Vagins, "this is what I risked my life for when I went before that anti-Semitic mob and told them, 'Before you touch any of my Jewish brothers, you will crucify me first.'"

"Well, Father, like you say, God acts in strange ways."

At that moment, a hospital administrator came into the waiting room. "Dr. Bushkin," she said, "please come up stairs." Without saying a word, he took the elevator to the second floor.

Sasha was being wheeled down the hall on her back and the baby was lying on her stomach, looking all around. The child, like Sasha, had dark hair and a complexion that matched his mother's swarthiness.

Levi and Sasha looked at each other in disbelief as the baby stared toward the light and began to cry.

"What a pair of lungs," Levi said. "Yes, that's our baby. Yelling and screaming must be an inherited trait.

"Sasha, let me go down and tell the others."

As he left the elevator and entered the waiting room, he told the group, "Our son has been delivered. Mother, child and father have never been better."

Hearty "Mazel tovs" rang out in the waiting room. Levi exchanged hugs and handshakes with the males, and kissed the females present.

He turned to the group and said, "This is the greatest thing that has ever happened to me."

The group soon left, with Levi following.

After his morning class, Levi returned to the hospital, early in the afternoon. The baby lay beside Sasha, sleeping.

Sasha said to him, "You know we never finished discussing whether we are going to stay in Ugograd and how we are going to live and raise the baby."

He then lifted up the baby, rocked him gently in his arms, and kissed his fleshy, bulbous cheek. As he handed the baby back to Sasha, he said, "We will name our son Abraham."

With that, he exited the hospital room and began a deep, emotional cry. When he returned to his apartment that evening, he wrote the next passage in his memoir: "Sasha and I have a son. He is a beautiful baby. Today I named him Abraham. After I left the baby and mother, I cried emotionally, like never before. But what I didn't know was whether I was crying tears of sorrow or tears of joy."

*Mark Carp*